Ethics, Economics and the State

Ethics, Economics and the State

Alan P. Hamlin

Lecturer in Economics
University of Southampton

St. Martin's Press
New York

© Alan P. Hamlin, 1986

All right reserved. For information, write:
Scholarly & Reference Division,
St. Martin's Press, Inc., 175 Fifth Avenue, New York, NY 10010

First published in America in 1986

Printed in Great Britain

ISBN 0–312–26547–6

Library of Congress Cataloging-in-Publication Data

Hamlin, Alan P., 1951–
  Ethics, economics and the state.

  Bibliography: p.
  Includes index.
  1. Economics—Moral and ethical aspects.
2. State, The. 3. Economics—Philosophy. 4. Political
science—Philosophy. 5. Welfare economics. I. Title
HB72.H33 1986   330   86–101–79

ISBN 0–312–26547–6

For Jan, for Beth

Contents

Preface

The subjects of this book are fundamental to welfare economics. Rational behaviour, ethical criteria and the justification and evaluation of social institutions will all be discussed, if usually rather briefly, in any welfare economics textbook. However, the approach adopted here is not constrained to welfare economics and is intended to range much more widely in exploring the relationships between ethics, economics and the state. The discussion lies at the current frontiers of economics, political philosophy and ethics. I am, by training, an economist, and the book reflects this by taking the mainstream economic position as the starting point for discussion. But I have deliberately eschewed all economic technique and formalism, and drawn widely from the contemporary, non-economic literature in developing the themes and in subjecting the economic orthodoxy to criticism. In this sense I hope that this book is a genuine step towards bringing together the approaches of distinct disciplines, rather than an example of the imperialist tendency in economics. In a discussion of social justice in the *New York Times* (3 January 1982) James Tobin claimed that "there's nothing more dangerous than a philosopher who's learned a little bit of economics", to which Robert Nozick replied, "unless its an economist who hasn't learned any philosophy". I hope that I have escaped Nozick's response in what follows; the relationship between economics and philosophy is too fundamental to allow complete specialisation.

I have tried to develop arguments which are sometimes subtle and complex in a style which is accessible to the non-specialist reader. The book could be read as an introduction to the subject area by anyone coming to the debate for the first time from any of the branches of social science. Providing

a view of the contemporary literature is an important aim of
the book; but it is not an exhaustive survey, neither is it
explicitly a textbook. Both in the presentation of arguments
and in the detailed arguments and criticisms themselves,
there is an element of novelty which, I hope, will be of
interest to the more specialist reader. I am sure that many
readers will find some sections of the discussion obvious,
oversimplified and naive; whilst perhaps finding other sections obscure, complex and sophisticated. My only defence
against this charge is that different readers will identify
different sections under each heading. In attempting to cover
a relatively broad range of material in a book of manageable
proportions I have inevitably had to limit the level of detailed
argument in many places. The reader should be aware from
the outset that many of the arguments offered are suggestive
rather than conclusive in nature.

This book has evolved very considerably in the process of
drafting, and no one shares my responsibility for its final
content or presentation. However, I have learned much of
what I understand in this area from listening to and talking
with many colleagues — economists and non-economists —
who in many cases were unaware of the existence of this
book but who nevertheless influenced its development. Some
of these debts are insufficiently acknowledged in what
follows, and I would particularly like to thank John Aldrich,
Geoffrey Brennan, John Broome, Allen Buchanan, James
Buchanan, Guido Calabresi, Jules Coleman, David Gauthier, Gilbert Harman, Alan Ingham, Anthony Kronman,
Loren Lomasky, Mancur Olson, Thomas Schelling, Amartya
Sen, Gordon Tullock, Alistair Ulph and Jack Wiseman. I
also thank two anonymous readers whose comments on the
penultimate draft have certainly improved both the book and
my understanding, even though I did not accept all of them.
At the institutional level, the project which became this book
was begun whilst I was a visitor at the Center for Study of
Public Choice, and the book has been completed whilst
visiting the Australian National University. I thank both
for their hospitality. Southampton University provided the
setting for the bulk of the work and I owe particular thanks
to Amanda Kibble at Southampton and Jan Anthony and
Joan O'Neill at the ANU who have worked miracles with
word processors.

1 Introduction

Individually rational behaviour may or may not produce collectively desirable results. If it does not, it may be possible to improve the situation by constraining individual behaviour within particular rules. These rules and their associated institutions together form a "state". This book is devoted to exploring the implications of these three apparently simple sentences which even a moment's reflection reveal to be riddled with uncertainties, ambiguities and imprecision. Amongst the questions which must be confronted are: what constitutes individual rationality? ; what view of collective desirability is to be taken? ; what are the links between these two questions? ; how is the institutional structure of the "state" influenced by views of rationality and desirability? ; and how might we expect states to vary as between alternative ethical stances?

A preliminary question concerns the definition and usage of the term "state". Throughout this book I take the state to be the authoritative institutional framework of society, so that the state consists of a set of authoritative institutions and procedural rules which, taken together, form the structural environment within which individuals operate and interact. This usage of state is of course rather broader than that commonly used in such phrases as "state-owned" or "state intervention" where the state is identified with government. In the broader view, government is just one possible social institution which forms a part of the overall state. Equally, the present usage of state should be distinguished from the views of the state as agent and of the state as a set of persons; where these ideas are used I will introduce alternative terminology. An "authoritative

1

institution" is one which is both powerful and potentially coercive in its relationships with individuals, so that individuals must, de facto, accept these institutions as real influences on their behaviour. That individuals recognise some authority in the institutional structure of society does not, of course, imply that those individuals necessarily approve of that authority. Many institutions are not authoritative in this sense and so do not form a part of the basic structure of society, or of the state. The logical relationship between the authoritative institutions of state and these lesser institutions will be discussed in Chapter 4.

The view of the institutions of state as devices which relieve the tension between individuals and the collective is, of course, not the only one possible; nor is it necessarily the view which accords most closely with the actual historical development of states. The state can alternatively be seen as being entirely dictatorial in nature, with one individual or group imposing rules and institutions on others without reference to any notion of collective desirability. As already noted, all states — whatever their justification or history — must have some authority if they are to impinge on individual behaviour; but the imposed, dictatorial state simply reflects the pre-existing power of the ruling individual or group and attempts to legitimise it by laundering the dictator's demands in the cleansing rhetoric of institutional authority. If a state is to be more than a disguise for the power of a dictator, it must base its authority not on some pre-existing power source but on some alternative source which derives ultimately from a particular ethical view and the realisation that the ethically desired outcome may not be guaranteed in the absence of the authoritative institutions of state.

The discussion of this book centres on alternative ethical justifications of state, but the intention is not simply to provide a range of alternative histories of actual states. It is rather to offer a critical discussion of alternative rationales of state which may be used to evaluate current institutions, whatever history might indicate about their actual origins.

The study of the tension between the individual and the collective, between rationality and ethics, which lies at the heart of our discussion, can be introduced and illustrated most simply in terms of the theory of games and, in particular, the class of games known as the prisoners' dilemma.[1] The simplest case of the prisoners' dilemma arises when two agents face a choice between just two strategies, where the pay-off to each agent depends not only on the agent's own choice but also on that of the other agent, in the manner illustrated in Table 1.1.

Here, each agent faces a choice between competing and cooperating with the other, and the relevant pay-offs are shown such that (2, 12), for example, indicates a pay-off of 2 to agent 1 and 12 to agent 2. Faced with this game, each agent has a private incentive to compete, since, whatever strategy is adopted by the other agent, competing will always produce a higher pay-off than cooperating. Competition is each individual's dominant strategy. We would therefore expect both agents to compete, with the result being pay-offs (5, 5). The nature of the "dilemma" is then that both agents would prefer to move to a position of mutual cooperation so as to achieve pay-offs (10, 10), but this move is prevented by each agent's fear that the other will exploit the preferred cooperation by competing and so capturing a still larger private pay-off. In the absence of any further device which might remove the dilemma, each agent will be confirmed in the strategy of competition even though each fully understands the nature of the game and the benefits of mutual cooperation.

Various approaches to the resolution or avoidance of the prisoners' dilemma have been discussed. The first, which

Table 1.1: The Standard Prisoners' Dilemma

		Agent 2	
		Cooperate	Compete
Agent 1	Cooperate	(10,10)	(2,12)
	Compete	(12,2)	(5,5)

might be termed the moral approach, is based on a line of
argument which suggests that whilst it may superficially
appear rational to compete in the setting of the game illustrated above, the realisation that this will not produce the
collectively desired outcome should be sufficient to convince
each agent that moral behaviour — ie, that behaviour
which, if adopted by all would lead to the desirable outcome — is in fact rational. This approach then tries to
close the gap between individual rationality and collective
desirability by the most direct route of denying the existence
of the gap, claiming that it is in fact rational to behave
morally. The most obvious example of this position is provided by the Kantian principle that each should do only
what (s)he could rationally will that all do.

The moral approach, as sketched, is of course seriously
incomplete since, although it argues that it is rational to
behave morally, it does not offer a precise criterion of what
morality demands. This points to the possibilty of many
variants of the moral approach. Nevertheless, it is clear that
all variants of this approach abolish the prisoners' dilemma
by extending the notion of individual rationality, and it is
equally clear that they abolish the possibility of any argument for a state which depends upon the state's ability to
encourage or enforce ethically desirable behaviour.

A second approach to avoiding the prisoners' dilemma
involves viewing the game illustrated above as merely one
round or stage in a continuing or repeated game, where
each agent expects to meet the other in the same situation
many times.[2] This repetition of the game provides the agents
with importantly different incentives, since it is now possible
to think of cooperation in the first round of the game as a
strategy intended to generate "trust" or "a reputation for
cooperation" which can be expected to pay dividends later
in the sequence of games as the other agent responds.
Indeed, if both parties seek to invest in a reputation for
cooperation in the first round, we can clearly expect that
the collectively desirable outcome of mutual cooperation
will occur from the outset.

Two aspects of this approach are of particular interest in
the present context. The first is that the argument depends

on a particular view of individual rationality and the way it extends through time. The second is that the argument operates entirely within the structure of the extended game. The agents' incentives, and hence their behaviour, are changed solely because of the repeated nature of the game and there is no recourse to any agency or device outside the game. This second aspect suggests that this approach can be termed the self-supporting, or self-enforcing, approach.

In terms of the state, this approach corresponds to a fully consensual view which argues that each individual recognises the long-term benefits to be gained from acting together, so that each individual voluntarily joins in a fully self-supporting society. At first glance it might be thought that this provides a view of anarchic society in which there is no place for an authoritative state at all, but it is easy to imagine that a self-supporting society will find it convenient and advantageous to erect administrative institutions which would have all the appearance of the machinery of state. What is, however, clear is that whatever institutions may arise, the fundamental authority of those state institutions would be grounded in the direct consensus of the members of society. In this view, the state is but a thin disguise through which society supports itself.

A third general approach to the prisoners' dilemma appeals directly to external devices in its attempt to escape from the dilemma, and so represents an enforcement approach. In its simplest form the appeal might be to the device of a binding contract between the agents which embodies an agreement to cooperate within the game. Of course, such a contract would have to specify a penalty for reneging in such a way as to ensure that each agent has a private incentive to abide by the contract — in our example a penalty of 3 would be sufficient — and also provide an assurance of enforcement, and both of these properties imply the existence of a third party or umpire with very particular powers. In short, this approach sets the prisoners' dilemma in the context of a wider set of institutions which allow the agents to escape from the dilemma by means of precommitting themselves to cooperative behaviour in a way that is plausible in the eyes of the other agent.

The external agency acting over and above the individual provides a clear model for the institutions of state. The state, in this view, embodies a real and independent authority which is necessary to ensure or promote socially desirable outcomes. The state is not fully consensual in that it cannot be seen simply as the product of cooperative action, but nevertheless one possible means of generating such a state would be via a prior agreement of the members of society in a form of social contract expressing the "general will". Despite this possibility of a social contract underlying the state, the state's authority does not derive from the direct consensus of the population. Indeed, a classic part of the function of such a state is to override individual choices in certain cases in order that the individual may be "forced to be free". In this view of the state, its authority derives directly from a notion of the general will or ethic which allows the state to override or constrain individual rationality.

So far our discussion of the prisoners' dilemma has provided three possible positions regarding the state. In the first approach, society is populated by moral individuals and so no additional institutional structure can be required on purely ethical grounds. In the second approach, the time dimension of society provides individuals with a private incentive consistent with the relevant ethic so that, again, no formal state is required — although it may be advantageous to erect institutions to administer society. The third approach provides us with a state which has independent authority and power, but which is devoted entirely to the pursuit of a particular vision of the general will.[3] The three approaches each involve a particular treatment of rationality. The first extends rationality to morality, the second extends it over time, and the third constrains it within rules. These views of the state do not exhaust the possibilities, and a return to the basic nature of the prisoners' dilemma can yield further insights.

As we have stressed, the basic problem underlying the prisoners' dilemma is that each individual acting in his own interest defeats the interest of all individuals taken together. Therefore to establish a prisoners' dilemma we need just three ingredients: a conception of the individual's interest, a conception of the collective interest interpreted as an ethical criterion, and a situation in which the two are held in tension. In the case of the dilemma illustrated in Table 1.1 it was (implicitly) assumed that the individual's interest lay in maximising his own pay-offs without regard to the pay-off of the other agent, whilst the general will was defined in terms of simultaneous increases in the pay-offs to all agents. If we interpret the numbers representing pay-offs in this example as utility measures, then this situation represents the familiar economist's assumptions that each individual maximises his own utility and that the general will can be operationalised as the Pareto criterion.

Utility maximisation and the Pareto criterion are, however, very particular models of rationality and ethics respectively, and the general significance of the prisoners' dilemma extends far beyond these specific theories of individual and general interests. For example, retaining the notion of utility maximisation as the relevant individualistic motivation, we might specify classical utilitarianism as the appropriate ethic. Looking back at Table 1.1, and interpreting the pay-offs now as cardinal utilities, we can confirm that the depicted situation is, once again, a genuine prisoners' dilemma. But now consider Table 1.2(a). Here we have a situation where the pay-offs are again to be interpreted as cardinal utility measures, and where individual utility-maximising behaviour implies that each individual will choose the dominant competitive strategy. These individually rational decisions will again yield the pay-off (5, 5), which is clearly an inferior outcome in terms of the utilitarian rule. But in this case the utilitarian ethic does not require mutual cooperation since aggregate utility is maximised where one agent competes whilst the other cooperates.

The case illustrated in Table 1.2(a) is a genuine, if modified, prisoners' dilemma since individual rationality defeats the collectively desirable outcome judged by the appropriate ethical criterion, but the resolution in this case cannot lie in finding a means of encouraging or enforcing mutual cooperation.[4] In the one-shot version of this game the solution requires the introduction of some asymmetry between agents even though the game itself is fully symmetric. One means of adding the required asymmetry would be to install external institutions which grant one agent some form of power over the other.

If the game is repeated, however, a further possibility arises. The symmetry of the game implies that a cooperative alternation of (2,20) and (20,2) is not only a desirable out-come on the utilitarian criterion, but also a Pareto optimum. This convergence of utilitarian and Paretian criteria is a very special property as can be seen from Table 1.2(b), which illustrates a similar modified prisoners' dilemma which lacks the full symmetry of Table 1.2(a). In this case the utilitarian resolution of the dilemma must involve the pay-off (30, 2) in every play of the game and so must act to the disadvantage of agent 2 relative to the rational equilibrium at (5, 5).

Here, then, is a further conception of the state as an instrument of one social group or class which is set in a

Table 1.2: The Modified Prisoners' Dilemma

(a) *The Symmetric Case*

		Agent 2	
		Cooperate	*Compete*
Agent 1	Cooperate	(10,10)	(2,20)
	Compete	(20,2)	(5,5)

(b) *The Asymmetric Case*

		Agent 2	
		Cooperate	Compete
Agent 1	Cooperate	(10,10)	(2,20)
	Compete	(30,2)	(5,5)

position of power over others. In our example the private interest of the powerful agent corresponds with the collective interest defined in terms of utilitarianism, and this indicates that even such an apparently dictatorial view of the state *may* be derived from a consideration of the relevant ethical criterion.

Table 1.2 provides examples which are prisoners' dilemmas under the assumption of utilitarianism and are also prisoners' dilemmas under the alternative ethical assumption of the Pareto criterion. The basic nature of the tension between individual rationality and the particular ethic is the same under each interpretation, but the response to the two interpretations may be widely divergent. In particular, each interpretation may provide the basis for a claim that the introduction of a state will provide a means of furthering collective ends and so provide an escape from the trap implied by the unrestrained pursuit of individual rationality; but the nature, constitution and institutional structure of the implied state will obviously depend markedly upon which interpretation of ethics is accepted.

As we have already noted, neoclassical welfare economics proceeds on the basis of the assumption of utility maximisation as the relevant notion of individual rationality whilst the criterion of social desirability actually utilised ranges from the Pareto criterion to a number of variants of utiliarianism; but it is in terms of the Pareto criterion that the most basic results are expressed.[5] Thus, the fundamental theorem of welfare economics demonstrates the conditions under which individually rational actions can be relied upon to produce a Pareto optimal outcome. This theorem serves both to legitimise rational behaviour as being socially desirable, and to justify a variety of types of government intervention aimed at improving the environment within which individual choices are made by means of correcting a range of market failures.

This sketch suggests the particular set of linkages between rationality, ethics, government policy and the economic environment which underlies neoclassical welfare economic analysis. However, each of these four basic elements is controversial, and in each case the staple neoclassical position has been the focus of considerable criticism emerging (or, more accurately, re-emerging) both from within economics and from other related disciplines.

The limitations of the standard utility-maximization assumption as a cogent view of individual rationality have increasingly been debated, whilst there has been a resurgence of interest in a variety of non-Paretian and non-utilitarian ethics and their relationship to economics. These debates will form the bases of Chapters 2 and 3 below. At the same time, the economic analysis of government has been shifting away from the mechanistic application of the simple neoclassical model which casts government in the role of an impersonal, monolithic and benign dictator, and towards a view which recognises government as an arena in which individuals, pressure groups, political parties and bureaucrats interact. In this view, each group may be expected to pursue different interests, with government policy emerging as the result of the trade-off between these interests in the contexts of institutional and procedural rules.

The social and structural environment in which individuals and governments operate has also received renewed attention. In the neoclassical view this environment is largely unexplained (except in so far as it is given by technology and the laws of physics). The social and institutional environment is taken to be predetermined and inviolate, acting as a sort of backdrop. The mechanistic view of government is entirely representative of the lack of detailed discussion of the formation and maintenance of social institutions within the mainstream neoclassical tradition. More recently, economists have returned to the attempt at understanding and explaining the pattern of institutional structures which include government and which collectively form the state. These attempts vary significantly, with some stressing the power of individuals to change their environment and others emphasising the evolutionary nature of change and arguing that it lies outside the deliberate control of any coherent group. But all stress the interaction between individuals' interests, the institutional structure and the design of policy. This area of debate is discussed in Chapter 4.

In its structure, this book mirrors the threefold distinction between individual rationality, ethics and the state. Chapter 2 presents the neoclassical view of rationality in some detail and then proceeds to review the critical debate which surrounds that position. Section 2.3 contains an overview of this debate and also provides an introduction to the remainder of the chapter, which develops some aspects of the debate on rationality in greater detail.

Chapter 3 begins with outlines of each of five major schools of ethical thought, including those which are most frequently used to ground economic analysis. Each of these sections is intended to summarise the particular approach and to note some of the major contemporary lines of argument for and against each view taken separately. Once the five views have been presented, the remainder of the chapter is devoted to discussion of the alternative views in an attempt to place each relative to the others, to view their relative strengths and weaknesses, and to suggest a framework which allows for some integration between the various approaches whilst simultaneously focussing on the major questions which divide them.

Chapter 4 then brings together the discussion of rationality and ethics to consider various views of the state which may result from the tension between any particular conceptions of these two forces. The implications for the institutional structure of society under these alternatives are discussed, as are the alternative views of the relationship between the individual and the community which gives rise to the role of politics. A fuller guide to the content of Chapter 4 is offered in Section 4.1. A retrospective overview of the major line of argument developed throughout the book can be found in Chapter 5.

2 Individual Rationality

2.1 PRELIMINARY IDEAS

What might we mean when we say that an action or decision made by an individual is rational? A detailed discussion of this question would require at least a book, and must remain beyond our present scope; [1] however, it is important to sketch some of the ideas which would appear in any more thorough discussion of rationality so that we may use these ideas in considering the neoclassical economists' view of rationality and the debate which surrounds it, which form the main topics of this chapter.

The key elements in any analysis of rationality would include the individual's beliefs, desires and decisions. Indeed, rationality is normally defined in terms of particular properties of one or more of these three elements, or their interrelationships. The individual's beliefs are beliefs concerning all aspects of the true nature of the world. In different words, the individual's beliefs constitute a model of the world which is currently accepted and which forms an introspective test-bed upon which alternative actions may be simulated.

Desires, on the other hand, represent the individual's ends, and provide an important driving force in any decision-making process. In conjunction with the model provided by beliefs, the individual's desires provide the evaluative criteria by which alternative actions may be compared. Finally, the individual's decisions are the outcome of a process of choice which may involve the interaction of the model of beliefs and the criteria of desires.

In this context it is relatively straightforward to identify three distinct interpretations of individual rationality, each of which provides a possible answer to our initial question, and each of which corresponds to an aspect of the everyday meaning of the word rational. The first interpretation can be approached in either of two ways. In one approach, this view of rationality concerns only the ultimate decisions of the individual, regardless of his beliefs and desires. Here the condition of rationality lies in the absence of mutually contradictory decisions. Consistency of actions is the hall-mark of this interpretation of rationality, and in this approach no reference need be made to desires or beliefs except to require that they are constant.

The second approach to this interpretation of rationality focusses attention on the interrelationship between beliefs and desires within the process of choice. In this approach rationality is defined as efficiency in pursuing given desires in the context of given beliefs. An argument linking effici-ency of choice with consistency of choice will be sketched in the setting of the neoclassical economist's view of rationality (Section 2.2)', and this argument establishes that these two approaches are fully equivalent. This first interpretation of rationality as consistency/efficiency I shall label means-rationality, indicating that, in this view, rationality is con-cerned with the formal properties of decision-making rather than the substantive content of decisions.

The second interpretation of rationality is as a condition on the beliefs of the individual which carries no direct implications for either desires or decisions. In this view, rationality is satisfied if the individual's set of beliefs about the real world embody scientific thought and the rules of logic. Thus an individual is rational to the extent that his internal model of the world is accurate and well-informed.

An example may help to clarify this interpretation. A primitive tribesman performing a rain-dance may be labelled irrational in this view, not because the dance is in itself irrational, nor because the tribesman's desire for rain is in any way irrational, but because the tribesman is acting on the basis of a belief-model which includes a causal link between rain-dancing and rain, when this link is denied by science as having no (logical or "rational") basis.

This interpretation of rationality, which I shall refer to as belief-rationality, opens up the relativism debate concerning the appropriate standpoint for making inter-personal, cross-cultural or inter-temporal comparisons of behaviour. Again this debate lies largely outside our scope; however, it will be useful to distinguish between two variants of the belief-rationality view.[2] The first and more stringent variant requires that rationality depend upon the belief-model being objectively true in all relevant respects. This objective belief-rationality view would condemn all actions based on mistaken, but genuinely held, beliefs as irrational. The second and milder variant, subjective belief-rationality, incorporates a relativist position by identifying as rational all actions based on genuinely held beliefs.[3]

The third interpretation of rationality which follows from the belief–desire–decision framework relates exclusively to the individual's desires. This view — which I shall term ends-rationality — covers a wide range of detailed positions which have in common the claim that some ends or desires are rational whilst others are not. The various positions differ in precisely which ends are to be deemed rational. This debate will be taken up later.

The three interpretations of rationality outlined here are neither mutually exclusive nor collectively exhaustive. As I have hinted, each interpretation conceals an active debate and we shall have some need to return to these debates in due course; nevertheless the alternative conceptions of rationality — and the associated terminology — do provide a basic framework which will be of value in characterising the view of rationality embedded in the neoclassical approach to economics and in discussing criticisms and extensions of that view. It is to this task that we now turn.

2.2 RATIONALITY IN NEOCLASSICAL ECONOMICS

The view of rationality which lies at the heart of neoclassical economics is often referred to simply as utility-maximis-ation. However, this description is both insufficient and potentially confusing since the phrase "utility-maximisation" is used in two distinct senses which relate to two different interpretations of rationality. In fact neoclassical economics embodies examples of all three interpretations of rationality discussed in the previous section, although emphasis is most often placed on the means-rationality and ends-rationality aspects, with belief-rationality rather hidden from view.

Consistency/efficiency of choice, or means-rationality, is most famously demonstrated in the theory of revealed preference. Here, an individual whose choices and actions reveal consistency is said to be rational regardless of the content of his choices. The link between simple consistency and efficiency of choice and, therefore, one sense of utility-maximisation is provided by the result that *any* consistent set of preferences can be represented as a utility function with the individual's choices indicating maximal utility. As Sen notes:

If you are observed to choose x rejecting y, you are declared to have "revealed" a preference for x over y. Your personal utility is then defined as simply a numerical representation of this "preference", assigning a higher utility to a "preferred" alternative. Within this set of definitions you can hardly escape maximising your own utility except through inconsistency. (Sen, 1977, p. 322)

Utility-maximisation used in this sense is then a purely formal specification of individual motivation having no substantive implications for the content of individual preference or desires.[4] This is not to imply that means-rationality in this context is in any way an empty concept. Indeed, the consistency requirement provides many insights into economic behaviour. However, the formal aim of acting consistently can tell us nothing about the substantive aims which actually motivate the individual's action since,

... if you are consistent, then no matter whether you are a single minded egotist or a raving altruist or a class conscious militant, you will appear to be maximising your own utility in this enchanted world of definitions. (Sen, 1977, p. 323)

If means-rationality is the only type of rationality that is allowed, the status of utility-maximisation is entirely restricted to the "as if" methodological position. The assumption that individuals act "as if" maximising their utility certainly allows predictions of individual behaviour to be made (on the additional assumption of unchanging desires and beliefs), but there would be no descriptive content to the notion of utility, which would be simply a convenient fiction.

Given these comments, it might seem that means-rationality, taken by itself, is unlikely to play a major role in any discussion of the source of state authority or in the evaluation of alternative institutional structures. Certainly, the prisoners' dilemma formulation appears to require a more substantive theory of rationality. However, as we shall see (Section 3.8), some views of ethics are argued to depend only on means-rationality, so that Rawls, for example, deliberately disavows any particular notion of ends-rationality in suggesting that individuals in the "original" position should be thought of as:

> . . . rational and mutually disinterested. This does not mean that the parties are egoists, that is individuals with only certain kinds of interests. . . . Moreover, the concept of rationality must be interpreted as far as possible in the narrow sense, standard in economic theory, of taking the most effective means to given ends. (Rawls, 1971, pp. 13–14.)

Ends-rationality in neoclassical economics provides us with the second sense of utility-maximisation. Perhaps the most frequently quoted statement of the particular form of ends-rationality in economics is provided by Edgeworth,[5] who wrote:

> . . . the first principle of economics is that every agent is actuated only by self-interest. (Edgeworth, 1881, p. 16)

Here then, utility-maximisation takes on a substantive form and becomes the conscious aim of individuals rather than a merely convenient description of consistent behaviour. Of course, utility-maximisation is a special case of the more general self-interest theory and, as such, it imposes additional restrictions. Most importantly in the present context, utility-maximisation must assume that all "interests" are commensurable into a single dimension — utility — so that in choosing among actions the individual need only compare the utility content of alternatives. Commensurability is more frequently discussed in the context of the utilitarian ethic — and we shall discuss it in more detail in Chapter 3 — so for the moment it is sufficient to note that egoism, or self-interest, and commensurability are both required components of utility-maximisation in its interpretation as a form of ends-rationality.

In addition to commensurability, we may identify six principal characteristics of the ends-rational view of utility-maximisation:

(i) It is *personal* in the sense that the utility to be maximised is my own. Other individuals do not enter into the evaluation process except possibly as "intermediate products" in the supply of external effects. Thus, I may derive utility from your actions (or inactions), but I am concerned about you only to the extent that my utility is involved.

(ii) It is *global* in the sense that the rational individual is capable of engaging in planning of the "one step backwards, two steps forward" variety.[6] Thus, given the individual's beliefs we can expect him to achieve a global maximum of utility, rather than be trapped at a local maximum determined by the sequence in which decisions are confronted.

(iii) It is *inter-temporal* in the sense that the utility to be maximised is lifetime utility rather than instantaneous utility. This characteristic is not universally accepted, and we shall return to it briefly in Section 2.3.

(iv) It is *expectational* in the sense that if the individual's belief-model indicates uncertainty concerning the utility content of alternative actions, the individual will choose actions to maximise the mathematical expectation of utility.

(v) It is *consequentialist* in the sense that actions are judged solely and completely by reference to their consequences. In the case of utility-maximisation, relevant consequences are those which carry some implication for the individual's own utility.

(vi) It is *act-specific* in the sense that each particular
decision is approached independently, with each
action being evaluated on its own merits rather than
according to some predetermined rule which might
be expected to work well on average.[7]

Each of these characteristics of utility-maximisation seen
as a particular form of ends-rationality provides a focal
point for criticism and debate, and we will return to these
debates in subsequent sections.

The concept of belief-rationality embedded within neoclassical economics relates to the informational status of
individuals. In the simple world of introductory textbooks
where uncertainty is banished, perfect information is normally assumed in order to ensure that each individual has
the same belief-model of the world and, furthermore, to
guarantee that this shared belief-model corresponds exactly
to the objective truth. The perfect information "assumption" is, therefore, revealed to be a strong statement regarding belief-rationality; indeed, it enforces the most stringent
form of objective belief-rationality.[8]

Once uncertainty is allowed to enter the analysis the
perfect information "assumption" is pushed at least one
step backwards. In its strongest form, it again requires all
individuals to share the same, objectively true, probability
model of the world from which they derive commonly held
expectations concerning the future. The fact that this position is commonly referred to as the "rational expectations"
hypothesis indicates that it is indeed a statement of belief-
rationality essentially similar to that which labels the rain-
dancing tribesman irrational in our earlier example.

A weaker requirement in an uncertain world is the requirement of subjective belief-rationality which involves each
individual having a fully specified but subjective probability
model of the world. This subjectivism of beliefs is then on
a par with the traditional subjectivism of desires where
each individual has independent views as to precisely what
constitutes his self-interest.

It is possible to attempt to build a bridge between the
subjectivist and objectivist views of belief-rationality by use

of the concept of learning. Thus it can be argued that each individual updates his own subjective belief-model in line with new information that becomes available with the passage of time. Since all individuals are, in fact, observing the same world, this argument suggests that we may expect all subjective belief-models to converge on to the single, rational, objective model.

This line of argument depends, however, on the constancy through time of the underlying true model and, even if this is granted, full convergence could not be guaranteed except in the limit when uncertainty is fully dispelled. The passage of time may reveal new information but, equally importantly, it reveals new uncertainties, so that it is difficult to argue that the simple passage of time is likely to update all subjective belief-models in a way which even approximates to the strong rational-expectations model of objective belief-rationality.

A further interesting distinction of relevance to belief-rationality is drawn by Elster who contrasts *parametric rationality* with *strategic rationality* where:

The parametrically rational actor treats his environment as a constant, whereas the strategically rational actor takes account of the fact that the environment is made up of other actors and that he is part of their environment, and that they know this, etc. (Elster, 1984, p. 18).

Economists will clearly recognise the parametrically rational individual as one who holds "Nash conjectures" regarding the absence of interactions between his own actions and those of his fellow actors.

The distinction between parametric and strategic rationality clearly involves two alternative specifications of the belief-model of the individual with the proviso that the strategic individual's belief-model is a closer approximation to the objective truth than the parametric belief-model. Elster goes on to suggest that this distinction is of vital importance in viewing the link between individual rationality and collective desirability (collective rationality in Elster's terminology). Indeed Elster claims that "A necessary (but insufficient) condition for collective rationality is the transition to strategic thought" (1984, p. 18).

This seems misleading. Economics is replete with examples illustrating the possibility of agents holding Nash conjectures reaching an equilibrium which is Pareto efficient and hence (in one view relevant to Elster's discussion) collectively desirable (or rational). The perfectly competitive market is the classic example in which the interaction between individuals can be ignored by each individual without loss of collective rationality. Clearly then, strategic rationality is neither a necessary nor a sufficient condition for collective desirability (rationality). Of course this is not to deny that, in some situations, parametrically rational individuals will fail to reach a Pareto efficient equilibrium which may be attained by strategically rational individuals, but this depends upon the details of the situation, and no general claim that strategic rationality is a necessary condition for collective rationality can be sustained.

This point illustrates a more general point. Just as strategic-rationality is not a necessary condition for collective desirability, so objective belief-rationality is not necessary for collective desirability. It is possible to imagine worlds in which individuals hold subjective belief-models which are at variance with the objective truth, and yet act so as to generate collectively desirable outcomes.

In its simplest and most characteristic form, neoclassical economics embodies strict objective belief-rationality together with both senses of utility-maximisation which involve, as we have seen, statements of ends-rationality and means-rationality. These three elements of the neoclassical economist's view of rationality add up to the frequently caricatured picture of *homo economicus* as an omniscient, infinitely calculating, egoistical maximiser. However, we have also seen that each of these three elements of the overall view is itself composed of separately identifiable parts.

2.3 THE CRITICAL DEBATE

Each of the three basic elements of the neoclassical view of rationality provides several points of departure for the critical debate. The purposes of this section are to provide an overview of this debate, a preview of the conclusions to be drawn from it, and an introduction and motivation for the following sections, which explore some areas of the debate in rather more detail.

In very general terms, the neoclassical theory of rationality has been criticised on two major fronts. On the one hand, it is argued to be too demanding, whilst on the other hand it is held to be too restrictive: too demanding in the sense that individuals are required to perceive, evaluate and calculate with absolute precision, and too restrictive in limiting attention to narrow self-interest as the sole motivator of individual action. In terms of our earlier definitions, the former line of criticism relates most obviously to the means-rationality aspect of the neoclassical theory and suggests that some degree of inefficiency in the pursuit of given ends must be accepted within a view of rationality. The latter criticism relates much more directly to the ends-rationality component of the neoclassical view in arguing for the recognition of a broader class of possible motivators.

At the heart of the debate on means-rationality is the notion of "bounded rationality" most strongly associated with the work of Simon.[9] The central idea here is that individuals are inherently inefficient and so may be inconsistent in their actions, but that individuals may come to recognise their own limitations and undertake actions to circumvent them to the greatest possible degree. Two major questions arise in this context. First, can bounded rationality itself be seen as a result of fully rational decision-making at a higher level where individuals argue that it is rational to bound their own rationality? Second, how can an individual operating under bounded rationality be expected to respond to this constraint? I shall discuss these questions in Section 2.4 to provide a justification for the view that bounded rationality cannot be fully subsumed within neoclassical rationality, and to argue that the individual's reaction to boundedness can be expected to challenge elements of the particularly economic form of ends-rationality. More particularly, I shall suggest that both "satisficing" and "procedural rationality" can be understood as reactions to boundedness which deny the global, consequentialist and act-specific characteristics of neoclassical ends-rationality.

The discussion of boundedness exemplifies the more general notion of imperfect rationality and the possibility of individuals adopting behavioural strategies of a second-best, rationality-improving kind in order to offset, but not completely eliminate, their own irrationality. The problem of "weakness of will" will also be discussed briefly in Section 2.4 as a further example of imperfect rationality which carries similar implications for rationality-improving, second-best strategies which operate largely via precommitment.[10]

If imperfect rationality forms a major critical position in relation to means-rationality, then extended rationality can be argued to occupy a similar position with respect to the particularly neoclassical form of ends-rationality. The fundamental points in any version of extended rationality are that own utility is not the sole motivator of individual action, and that there exists an internal tension between self-interest and other rational goals. A view of extended rationality will be developed in Section 2.5 in the context of the debate on altruism which has traditionally provided a rich ground for criticism of self-interest theories of rationality. Again, the major questions to be considered will involve the possibility of incorporating apparently altruistic behaviour within a fully neoclassically rational view of enlightened self-interest, and the behavioural implications of the acceptance of an extended rationality viewpoint.

Given the major alternatives of imperfect and extended rationality, Section 2.6 will provide comparative application. The debate on the nature of rational choice under uncertainty will be viewed as a debate between neoclassical rationality, imperfect rationality and extended rationality in order to focus attention on these alternative views and their distinctive features. The debate on uncertainty will also allow some brief comments on the subjectivist critique of the use of rationality in economics.

Section 2.7 will then take the various notions of rationality and apply them in an area of direct relevance to our later

discussion — the individually rational reaction to the existence of institutional rules, rights and obligations.

The discussion contained in these sections will allow us
to consider criticisms aimed at almost all of the characteristics of the neoclassical position which were identified
in the previous section. The major exception is the inter-
temporal aspect of neoclassical ends-rationality which insists
that agents take a temporally neutral view of utility. There
are three distinct facets to the debate on this issues: the
first concerns the rationality of discounting future utility,
the second recognises that preferences may change through
time and raises the question of the rational reaction to such
anticipated changes, and the third concerns the process
of preference change and the question of whether some
preferences can be viewed as more rational than others.
Each of these questions is of considerable importance in its
own right but, in the present context, it will be sufficient
to sketch out the debate in the briefest possible way in
order to justify the view that the issues raised are essentially
similar to those already identified in the areas to be discussed in subsequent sections.

In discussing discounting we are concerned only with the
pure time-discounting of utility. All parties to the debate
are agreed that discounting in respect of uncertainty, or
discounting of, say, financial quantities may be entirely
rational. Pure time-discounting of utility is the issue, and
whether it is irrational to prefer utility in the near future to
utility in the further future is the stark statement of the
question.

Rawls speaks for many when he provides the affirmative
answer:[11]

We are to see our life as a whole, the activities of one rational subject
spread out in time. Mere temporal position, or distance from the present,
is not a reason for favouring one moment over another. Future aims may
not be discounted solely in virtue of being future. (Rawls, 1971, p. 420)[12]

However, the interpretation of the conflict between self-
interested rationality and discounting is still the subject of
debate. Two positions of particular importance may be

noted. Elster offers the interpretation of discounting as a symptom of imperfect rationality so that weakness of will is suggested as the source of the strictly irrational tendency to discount future utility.[13] Alternatively, Parfit suggests that the observation of discounting is an argument for an extended view of rationality, which holds not only that utility is utility whenever it occurs, but also that utility is utility whoever it occurs to.[14] This line of argument draws a parallel between a person at different times and different people — a parallel that we will meet again.

In this way the tension between the pure time-discounting of utility and neoclassical rationality can be seen as a further arena for the general debate between imperfect, extended and neoclassical theories of rationality.

The possibilities for precommitment are clear in the case of changing preferences. The individual at time 1 may pre-commit his actions at time 2 in such a way that the long-term outcomes are more appealing to the individual at time 1 than those which he envisages if, at time 2, he is free to act on changed preferences. The question is whether such precommitment is rational, or even rationality-improving in some second-best sense.[15] The individual at time 1 will believe that lifetime utility is increased by precommitment, whilst the individual at time 2 will believe that lifetime utility is decreased. Since they share the same lifetime, only one of them (at most) can be right, but which? Does temporal priority lend weight to earlier preferences and thereby justify all such precommitments? Or is there some presumption that preferences evolve in a way that may loosely be termed "progressive", so that all attempts at precommitment of this type should be labelled irrational?

The answers to these questions must lie in determining which preference changes can be viewed as progressive. If one had a yardstick, or meta-preference ranking, which was capable of determining the position of any particular preference ranking in some hierarchy, then one could always identify situations in which precommitment was rational, but in the absence of such a fixed yardstick no judgement can be made since the preference change renders the concept of a lifetime utility ill-defined.

The prospect of answering the questions of which changes in preferences are desirable and which may justifiably support strategies of precommitment depends upon finding a relevant and unchanging metric of desirability. This cannot be provided from within the framework of the neoclassical theory of rationality since the only metric within that view is based on preferences. Yet without some means of overcoming the difficulties encountered once changes in preferences are considered, it is difficult even to conceive of the lifetime utilities which lie at the heart of the neoclassical view. Neoclassical rationality is therefore in a double bind: without some external criterion of desirability it cannot satisfactorily ground the concept of lifetime utility, but if such an external criterion were admitted it would naturally challenge lifetime utility as a motivator of action.

Again then, the central elements of the discussion of these aspects of the inter-temporal dimension of rationality are the notions of precommitment and extended rationality which we have already identified for discussion in subsequent sections.

2.4 BOUNDED RATIONALITY

We have already noted that the major thrust of the notion of bounded rationality is the incorporation of human imperfection into a theory of rationality. The neoclassical view of means-rationality is fully acknowledged within the bounded rationality viewpoint, but its status is argued to be that of an ideal which individuals strive towards but can never reach, rather than a description of actual behaviour or a criterion of practical rationality. Bounded rationality therefore attempts to provide the basis for a positive theory of imperfectly rational behaviour whilst retaining full, unbounded means-rationality as the appropriate normative ideal.

The first major question to be confronted concerns the suggestion that bounded rationality can be reinterpreted in such a way that it can be fully subsumed within neoclassical rationality. The strategy of this argument is to focus attention on questions of the form "is it rational to be rational only if the benefits of rationality exceed the costs? " In order to view this debate we need to be rather more explicit about the nature of the constraints which bound rationality.

Simon (1954) identifies two major sources of constraints on rationality. Individuals may lack the ability to identity optimal actions given a particular belief-model and particular desires. Alternatively, they may lack information relevant to the decision in hand. Whether ability or information is constrained, a further distinction between exogenous and endogenous constraints is relevant.

An exogenous constraint is one which is outside the influence of the constrained individual. Thus an exogenous informational constraint is operative whenever an individual lacks not only relevant information but also any means of obtaining it. By contrast, an endogenous constraint arises in part as a result of the individual's own decisions. Thus, an endogenous informational constraint is operative whenever an individual lacks information and has decided not to take the actions necessary to gather it. Endogenous constraints are, by their nature, consciously recognised by the individual concerned, whilst exogenous constraints may be either recognised or not.

The attempt to subsume bounded rationality within neoclassical rationality focusses entirely on endogenous constraints and can be presented in terms of the idea of "rational ignorance". Here the argument is that an individual faces costs of information-gathering and, as a fully rational neoclassical man, will pursue that activity only to the point where marginal expected benefits are equal to marginal expected costs. The resulting position is then not the full information setting of simple neoclassical economics, but the "rational ignorance" or "optimal information" setting which recognises that information is itself a commodity. A similar argument can readily be constructed to correspond to the case of endogenous ability constraints; the "rational level of efficiency" would be the concept analogous to "rational ignorance".

This line of argument suggests that endogenous constraints on rationality are not constraints at all, but are more appropriately seen as the result of full rationality. However, whilst not denying the obvious truth that decisions regarding information-gathering are made, there is a question as to whether these decisions (or the analogous "rational inefficiency" decisions) can ever be *fully* rational, since the argument used involves a form of infinite regress.[16]

A decision to gather more information is made by comparing expected costs and benefits. Even in a world where uncertainty is modelled in the conventional manner, so avoiding the additional difficulties associated with a radically subjectivist interpretation of uncertainty (Section 2.6), such a comparison itself requires information. This second-stage information may already be incorporated into the individual's belief-model but, by assumption, the individual knows the model to be inaccurate in the very area of concern, so that it can hardly be fully rational to rely on the existing, inaccurate model to evaluate decisions intended to reform that model. Alternatively, the second-stage information may itself have to be gathered, raising the decision of whether or not to gather it, and the infinite regress beckons.

The attempt to incorporate bounded rationality within neoclassical rationality by arguing that it is rational to bound your own rationality is superficially attractive. However, it leaves exogenous constraints on rationality entirely out of account and, even in the area of endogenous constraints, it fails ultimately by failing to show that it is possible to cut through the infinite regress of rationally evaluating the decision to rationally evaluate the decision. . . .[17]

At a more fundamental level, however, this debate simply misses a major point underlying the idea of bounded rationality. This point is that individuals are *inherently* imperfect and are, therefore, psychologically incapable of being fully rational in the neoclassical sense. The question of whether a fully rational individual might voluntarily bound his own rationality is then irrelevant since the idea of such an individual is psychologically incoherent.

We may now turn to our second major question concerning an individual's reaction to his own boundedness. It is this recognition of limitation which may motivate a change of view of ends-rationality away from the maximising egoism

of the perfectly rational neoclassical man. The central argument here is essentially an application of the second-best
argument familiar in economics. In the present context, this
argument holds that if your ability is constrained or
bounded, the best you can do may involve setting yourself
targets different from those which would be appropriate in
the case of unconstrained ability.

The most obvious contender for such a second-best,
rationality-improving strategy is the adoption of a satisficing
objective in place of the neoclassically rational objective of
global maximisation. A satisficing objective may be defined
in terms of the dependence of choice on the sequence in
which alternatives are considered and the specification of a
criterion of acceptability. The satisficing rule is then simply
to adopt the first acceptable action which is considered.

There is a simple analogy here with a climber who proceeds on the satisficing basis of choosing compass bearings
at random until he finds one that points uphill; he then
climbs a set distance before repeating the process. Each
decision determines the site of the next decision. On a
simple hill, such a climber will eventually reach the global
peak, although his route will be inefficient; however, on a
more complex landscape the climber's final destination as
well as his route will be determined by the order in which
compass bearings are selected.

The significance of satisficing is that the individual
becomes unpredictable. In the context of our simple
climber, we cannot predict his direction of travel from any
point (unless there is only one compass bearing that points
uphill) nor his final destination (unless there is only one
local maximum). In the case of an individual in a game
situation, we cannot predict his choice of strategy without
two pieces of information which would be irrelevant to
the fully rational, neoclassical man. We require both the
individual's definition of "satisfactory" and the order in
which the alternative strategies are considered.

Table 2.1 provides an example of the potential impact of
satisficing. The pay-off matrix illustrated is fully symmetric
(as normal the pay-off (12, 3) indicates a pay-off of 12 for
agent 1 and 3 for agent 2) and it is easy to see that this

game is a version of the prisoners' dilemma. Strategy D is a dominant strategy — it maximises the agent's own pay-off whichever strategy is adopted by the opponent — if adopted by both agents, strategy D yields pay-offs (4, 4), whilst pay-offs (10, 10) are available if both agents choose strategy A. Now, if both agents in this game are satisficers it is possible to imagine that each would choose strategy A simply by considering strategies in an order which placed A before D, and by using a criterion of satisfaction which finds A acceptable. In this event, the individuals' irrationality saves them from the prisoners' dilemma.

This example is of a single or one-shot game, but even if the game is repeated the outcome (10, 10) may persist since the pay-off on the first play is "satisfactory" and is therefore unlikely to stimulate either agent to search for a new strategy. Once established, strategy A may prove to be stable.

Of course nothing guarantees that the satisficing agent will avoid the dominant strategy D in his initial search, and to add plausibility to the possibility sketched in this example a discussion of the way in which strategies are perceived is required. Some comments in this direction will be offered below; but, for the moment, the point to stress is that the very property of satisficing which makes it sub-optimal from the perspective of neoclassical rationality may in some cases allow satisficers to reach social positions inaccessible to fully rational maximisers. However, it should be noted that this argument works only if both (all) agents are satisficers. In

Table 2.1: Prisoner's Dilemma and Satisficing

		Agent 2			
		A	B	C	D
	A	(10,10)	(4,9)	(4,11)	(3,12)
Agent 1	B	(9,4)	(4,4)	(4,4)	(2,5)
	C	(10,4)	(4,4)	(4,4)	(2,5)
	D	(12,3)	(5,2)	(5,2)	(4,4)

a mixed world of satisficers and maximisers, the satisficers can expect to be exploited.

The perception of alternative strategies raises psychological questions well beyond the scope of this book, and so I will be content to make just one or two simple observations. First, some answers to questions are more obvious than other — equally true — answers. Thus, when asked to divide a cake in two, an "obvious" solution is to divide it equally; similarly, when asked if some hypothetical future situation is satisfactory it is "obvious" to use the status quo as a benchmark and answer 'yes' if the new situation is an improvement, even though the status quo may not be the truly relevant criterion. Obvious strategies may be those which are considered first by a satisficer with the search for non-obvious strategies undertaken only if no satisfactory obvious alternative can be found. The status quo and current social convention are obvious influences on what is obvious, and this provides an argument for continuity or stability. If social conventions suggest obvious strategies these will be chosen relatively often, thereby reinforcing the original convention. However, this reinforcement effect does nothing to identify which strategies/conventions are likely to arise.

One possibly relevant point here is that symmetry may play a part. The symmetric division of the cake, the equal treatment of others, etc, may appear as obvious possibilities because of their special symmetry or neutrality properties, and this may be enough to ensure that symmetric, egalitarian, non-discriminatory strategies are at least considered, so biasing upward their chances of being adopted by a satisficer.

Another source of "obvious" strategies in a repeated game situation is the observation of the strategies used by others. In the context of our earlier example, if agent 1 adopted strategy C (by considering only B and C) whilst agent 2 adopted strategy A (by considering A and B), we might expect each to consider the other's chosen strategy in the future. In this case such reconsideration would result in both agents choosing strategy A; but it is clear that this general line of argument points to the fact that a dominant strategy, if one exists, will be contagious, spreading through the population of agents once it is introduced. Such contagion may, of course, be slow so that if the game or the stock of agents evolve through time it may never complete its progress.

A second possible response to the recognition of boundedness involves the adoption of "procedural rationality", which effectively shifts attention from the act-specific evaluation of full neoclassical rationality to the adoption of a rule or procedure for decision-making which is expected to work well over a number of applications whilst avoiding both the costs of detailed evaluation and the basic inability to reach optimal decisions.

The adoption of procedural rationality involves a form of precommitment in that the individual commits himself to make future decisions of a particular type by reference to a specified rule of thumb. But this form of precommitment is not binding. The individual clearly reserves the right to deviate from the self-imposed rule if it becomes clear that the rule-directed behaviour is not appropriate in a particular case. All that the precommitment implies, in this type of case, is the statement of intent that no great effort will be expended in checking if the rule is appropriate in each instance.

This depiction of procedural rationality as a rationality-improving strategy arising out of boundedness and replacing act-specific evaluation captures the main force of Simon's classic line of argument.[18] However, an alternative line of argument is available which places procedural rationality relative to the consequentialist characteristic of neoclassical ends-rationality (Section 2.2). If aspects of actions other than their consequences (eg their inherent, procedural properties) are allowed to enter into an individual's motivation, then it follows that an individual may trade off substantive or consequential rationality against procedural rationality in making decisions. This view would fit well with the idea that many people apparently place great weight on whether a thing has been done "by due process" or "through the appropriate channels" as a source of value additional to the fact that the thing has in fact been done.

Each of these arguments provides a means of shifting

attention away from individual act evaluation in terms of consequential utility and towards internally prescribed, but non-binding, rules of behaviour which apply across many acts and which, in general, imply a utility loss relative to the perfectly rational case. The arguments differ in that whilst the first identifies procedural rationality as a strategy resulting from the individual's recognition of boundedness, the second places procedures alongside consequences as possible motivators, so that the individual would value procedural rules of behaviour not as strategic devices to some further end, but as ends in themselves.

Weakness of will, like bounded rationality, relates to a failure of rationality internal to the individual; but there are differences, as well as similarities, between the two issues.[19] The simplest example of weakness of will involves an individual making a plan concerning his intended action in some future situation, and then failing to implement that plan when the relevant situation arises. The central feature of the weakness-of-will case is the difficulty of implementing what is recognised as the rational plan rather than any difficulty in recognising the rational plan itself. Such weakness clearly points to an inefficiency internal to the individual and therefore relates to a failure of means-rationality which may result in inconsistent behaviour.[20]

Once again then we have a situation in which full neoclassical rationality is acknowledged as the appropriate normative ideal, and where a problem thrown up by human imperfection, which prevents fully rational decision-making at each moment in time, is absorbed into the analysis by means of allowing the individual to respond to the recognition of his own partial irrationality. This point is clearly made in Elster's discussion of Ulysses' instruction to have himself tied to the mast so as to avoid the temptation of the Sirens:

Ulysses was not fully rational, for a rational creature would not have to resort to this device; nor was he simply the passive and irrational vehicle for his changing wants and desires, for he was capable of achieving by indirect means the same end as a rational person could have realised in a direct manner. His predicament — being weak and knowing it — points to the need for a theory of imperfect rationality. (Elster, 1984, p. 36)

Elster suggests that Ulysses achieves the same end as could be achieved by a fully rational individual, but this is doubtful. Ulysses does, after all, have to suffer the cost of being lashed to the mast — a cost which a fully rational individual can easily avoid. It is more appropriate to cast the case in the language of the second best by arguing that Ulysses responds to the constraint on his rationality by investing in an irrational but low-cost action now (being tied to the mast) in order to avoid an irrational and high-cost action which he could foresee (steering on to the rocks).

As is illustrated by the case of Ulysses, the principal response to recognised weakness of will is to engage in some action designed to bind, precommit or pre-empt future choice of action. I have emphasised the point that the action of binding is itself irrational in the full neoclassical sense, whilst it is rationality-improving in the second-best sense. This can be seen clearly in the pay-off matrix shown in Table 2.2, which is typical of many weakness-of-will situations.

Table 2.2 depicts the decisions faced by a single individual over two periods ("now" and "later") and their associated pay-offs (where 0, 5) indicates a pay-off of 0 now and 5 later). The fully rational man clearly makes the Not Bind decision now, and the Bound decision later, but this strategy which defines fully rational behaviour is definitionally unavailable to a weak individual who can only take the Bound decision later if he take the Bind decision now. If the weak individual does not anticipate his own weakness he will act rationally now in making the Not Bind decision, but will then take the irrational Not Bound decision later. If the individual recognises his own weakness he can

Table 2.2: Weakness of Will

		Decision later	
		Bound	Not Bound
Decision Now	Bind	(0,5)	—
	Not Bind	(1,5)	(1,0)

improve on this outcome by adopting the irrational Bind decision now and rational Bound decision later.

The recognition of weakness allows the individual to choose the timing of his irrationality and therefore its cost, but he cannot escape his constraint altogether. It is also clear that the pay-offs in Table 2.2 could be rearranged so that the recognition of weakness would not lead to the choice of the Bind/Bound strategy if the costs of pre-commiting exceed the costs of failing to implement the rational plan later. Weakness of will always implies a loss of rationality, but only sometimes will it be rationality-improving to accommodate that loss.

In contrast to the discussion of the form of pre-commitment involved in the adoption of procedural rationality, the precommitment which characterises weakness-of-will cases must be binding on the individual in order to enforce the implementation of the rational plan. This distinction highlights two possible roles of precommitment — one as a signpost to action, and the other as an enforcement of action.

The general notion of imperfect rationality which encompasses bounded rationality and weakness of will is defined in terms of an inherent inability to be fully rational. It is therefore clear that a distinct version of imperfect rationality will exist for each separately identified theory of perfect rationality. The common thread that unites these particular theories of imperfect rationality lies in the possibility that individuals recognise their own limitations and engage in strategies designed to move them closer to full rationality. These strategies — of which satisficing, procedural rules of thumb, and the precommitment of future action have been discussed — are entirely internally generated responses to imperfection, but they carry social significance in at least two way. First, it is possible that such strategies lead to situations which are socially preferred to those which would result from fully rational decision-making. Since individual rationality may conflict with social desirability it should not be surprising that imperfect rationality may, in itself, be socially desirable. The second avenue to social significance recognises that rationality-improving strategies may often involve external agencies. Such external agencies may provide the least-cost means of ensuring binding precommitment, or may simply act as signposts to appropriate action. Such external agencies will form one avenue of approach to the analysis and justification of social institutions in our later discussions.

2.5 ALTRUISM

The apparent existence of altruism has been seen by many as a strong challenge to the neoclassical form of ends-rationality. The topic has been discussed repeatedly throughout the history of economics, but only recently has there been a sustained interest in the topic.[21] The first issue to be addressed in this section is the possibility that apparently altruistic behaviour can be incorporated within the neoclassical view of rationality. Having suggested that this is not a satisfactory response to the challenge of altruism, I will offer a discussion of the potential impact of "genuine", or non-self-interested, altruism in situations of the prisoners' dilemma type which will motivate the central idea of extended rationality as an alternative model.

We may identify three distinct lines of argument which attempt to reconcile apparently altruistic behaviour with neoclassical rationality. The first and most direct is based on the economics of externalities and simply claims that the "donor's" utility is positively related to the utility, income or consumption of the "recipient". The crucial point here is that the recipient is viewed entirely instrumentally by the donor so that an individual will behave "altruistically" only to the point where *his* marginal utility is equal to *his* marginal cost. The recipient's utility is simply a consumption good like any other seen from the point of view of the donor.

A severe difficulty confronting this line of argument lies in its inability to overcome the free-rider problem. Much apparently altruistic behaviour involves individual donors contributing to large charities or groups of recipients. The simple self-interest model of altruism suggests that each such potential donor faces the classic public good problem in which his own contribution increases his costs markedly whilst increasing the total income of the charity — and therefore his own utility — only marginally. The prediction of free-riding, and further predictions concerning donations to large charities, do not appear to fit the facts and this casts considerable doubt on the ability of this approach to explain more than a small part of observed altruism.[22]

A second possibility for claiming that altruism is, at base, self-interested is to argue that the act of giving itself produces utility. One version of this argument which seems to fit the analysis of repeated games is the claim that charitable behaviour may build a valuable reputation for the donor within a community. However, this type of argument is thin. Behaving altruistically can build a favourable reputation only if others are unaware of the underlying self-interest. For it to be possible to masquerade as an altruist and so gain kudos, it must be the case that genuine altruists exist and that the public cannot distinguish between real and bogus altruism. The possibility of bogus altruism depends on the widespread existence of real altruism and this real altruism is still unexplained.

Whilst this second line of argument does escape from the free-rider problem, it cannot provide a fully satisfactory explanation of altruism. Without a more satisfactory mechanism by which giving is translated into utility, the argument reduces to the *ad hoc* assertion that giving does increase utility, and whilst this defines altruism as self-interested it cannot be said to explain it.

The third possible method of incorporating altruism into rational egoism involves a more indirect, strategic or evolutionary appeal to self-interest.[23] The general idea of this line of argument is that whilst altruism may appear to be un-self-interested in the short-run, its long-term benefits — including the benefit of living in a society of altruists — may dominate these short-run costs even in the egoist's private calculus.

Put in these terms it is clear that the central problem facing this line of argument is, once again, the temptation to free-ride, since the best position for each individual is that of an egoist in an altrustic group. For altruism to be an evolutionary stable strategy in a society of individuals motivated by enlightened self-interest, some means of overcoming this free-rider problem has to be endogenously provided.[24]

This discussion brings us back to the structure of the prisoners' dilemma in which each individual recognises that altruism is better for all, but where the fully altruistic solution is prevented from arising by the individually dominant strategy of simple egoism. This then is the central paradox which lies at the heart of all attempts to explain altruism within self-interest: even if it is possible to argue that altruism will achieve increased personal utility for all, it is not generally possible to find a purely individualistic means of realising this outcome which is available to egoists.

Our discussion so far has concentrated on the attempt to incorporate altruism within egoism and, in summary, we may conclude that whilst some fraction of apparently altruistic behaviour may be explained by one or other of the appeals to egoism discussed above (as selfish altruism or bogus altruism), there remains an irreducible core of altruism which resists such incorporation. However, just as the prisoners' dilemma and the temptation to free-ride confront the self-interested altruist, so the genuine altruist provides a possible escape from the prisoners' dilemma.

This escape route involves the transformation of the prisoners' dilemma game, and the argument is best put in the context of a simple example. Under pure egoism each agent places total weight on his own utility pay-off, completely ignoring the pay-off of the other agent. A genuine altruist may however place some positive weight on another's utility even though it does not affect his own utility. Such an altruist may then be motivated by the weighted sum of his own utility and that of the other agent, where w identifies the weight placed on the other's utility, and $(1-w)$ the weight placed on own utility.

To illustrate this situation, Table 2.3 represents a standard prisoners' dilemma. In the context of this pay-off matrix we can now identify agent 1 as the altruist and let the value of w be equal to one-half, so that agent 1 is motivated equally by his own utility and that of agent 2. In these circumstances, the cooperative strategy is a dominant strategy for agent 1. Indeed, for the pay-off matrix in Table 2.3, this result follows whenever $w > 5/12$.[25] Whilst the numerical value of w required clearly depends upon the details of the game in question, the general point is that there is a level of altruism — interpreted as a value of w — sufficient to ensure that the altruist selects the cooperative strategy.

For values of w below this critical level, altruism by itself is insufficient to provide the basis for cooperation; however, we may still have a situation markedly different from the standard prisoners' dilemma. Any w such that $2/12 < w < 5/12$ transforms the game of Table 2.3 into an assurance game which is distinguished from a prisoners' dilemma by the fact that free-riding is not the most attractive option.[26] Table 2.4 indicates that the transformed matrix of pay-offs for the particular case of $w = 1/3$; of course it is no longer possible to interpret the pay-offs to agent 1 as own utilities, but they still represent his choice ordering.

From the point of view of altruistic agent 1, no dominant strategy now exists since his best strategy depends upon agent 2's strategy. In fact agent 1 will always wish to com-

Table 2.3: Prisoners' Dilemma and Altruism

| | | Agent 2 | |
		Cooperate	Compete
Agent 1	Cooperate	(10,10)	(0,12)
	Compete	(12,0)	(5,5)

Table 2.4: The Transformed Matrix

| | | Agent 2 | |
		Cooperate	Compete
Agent 1	Cooperate	(10,10)	(4,12)
	Compete	(8,0)	(5,5)

pete when agent 2 competes, and cooperate when agent 2 cooperates. How then should agent 1 actually behave if he cannot wait for agent 2 to reveal his strategy? If he could be fully assured of agent 2's choice, his problem is trivial, he simply follows suit; but in the absence of such complete assurance, it is often suggested that he should compete. For example Elster writes:

> With less than perfect information, he should use the maximin criterion and choose the strategy that guarantees him the highest minimum pay-off . . . in the Assurance Game the slightest uncertainty or suspicion will make an actor choose D (compete) rather than C (cooperate). (Elster, 1984, p. 21)

However, as argued by Collard (1978), assurance need not be complete in order for agent 1 to choose the cooperative strategy. If we let p indicate agent 1's subjective estimate of the probability that agent 2 will cooperate, so that $p = 1$ corresponds to the case of perfect (subjective) assurance, then agent 1 will cooperate if:[27]

$$p > 5/3 - 4w$$

So that, for example, if $w = 1/3$ agent 1 will cooperate provided that he believes that agent 2 will cooperate with a probability of at least 1/3. The greater is agent 1's altruism, the less assurance he requires to justify his own cooperation; with $w = 5/12$ he will cooperate even if he believes that agent 2 will certainly compete, whilst if $w = 2/12$ he would require full assurance before cooperating.

This discussion indicates that the degree of altruism is of considerable significance in determining the nature of its effect. At low levels ($w < 2/12$ in our example) altruism does not materially affect the situation, the altruist still confronts a prisoners' dilemma and his dominant strategy — even accounting for his altruism — is to compete. At moderate levels ($2/12 < w < 5/12$ in our example) altruism transforms the prisoners' dilemma into an assurance game but is not of itself sufficient to guarantee cooperative behaviour by the altruist — a degree of trust or assurance is still required. Finally, at high levels ($w > 5/12$ in our example) altruism is sufficient to ensure that cooperation is the altruist's dominant strategy.

Extending the individuals rationality beyond self-interest in this way provides a potential escape from the prisoners' dilemma and, more generally, changes the nature of the tension between rationality and ethics. Of course, in one sense it is always possible to argue that such extended rationality is formally equivalent to the reassertion of egoism. In our example we could write a "motivation function" for agent 1 of the form:

$$M_1 = (1 - w)U_1 + wU_2$$

where U_1 and U_2 identify the utilities of agents 1 and 2 respectively. Since agent 1 acts to maximise M_1 in our example, we could simply *define* this motivation function to be his "true" utility function and so insist that he is maximising his own utility. This would amount to incorporating altruism within egoism by the first argument discussed above.

All of this is true, and illustrative of the proposition that *any* consistent behaviour can be modelled as being derived from some appropriately defined utility function (the first sense of utility-maximisation discussed in Section 2.2). Nevertheless, this line of criticism misses the fundamental point that M_1 is *not* a utility function (in the second sense discussed in Section 2.2) and that utility is *not* the sole motivator. A point to note here is that the recognition of motivations other than own utility breaks the link between preference and behaviour, so that it can no longer be argued that action reveals preference.[28] The altruist may act in a way which reduces his own utility.

The particular illustrative example discussed above is clearly subject to the free-rider problem in any more general, n-person, setting. The question of whether the notion of extended rationality might effectively overcome this problem in the setting of altruism remains an open one. Some forms of extended rationality do seem to escape this trap — for example the "fair-share" argument of Margolis, the "reciprocity" argument of Sugden, or the Kantian moral view discussed by Collard.[29] The point here, as in the assurance game framework, is that pure altruism — a selfless concern for others — will only rarely and in extreme cases be sufficient to make any significant difference to individual behaviour. Only when altruistic concern combines with particular views regarding individual obligations and duties, or particular evaluations of the behaviour of others, will altruism be individually effective. In other words, altruistic concern has to be embedded in a more fully specified theory of extended rationality.

Perhaps the most promising line of attack on the specification of such extended rationality begins with the attempt to provide the individual decision-maker with a more detailed internal structure. Harsanyi distinguishes between an individual's "subjective preferences" which form the standard utility function, and his "ethical preferences" which "express what he prefers only in those possibly rare moments when he forces a special impartial attitude upon himself" (Harsanyi, 1955, p. 14). Sen (1974, 1977) has taken up this theme of multiple preference rankings within a single individual.

Sen's discussion centres on the distinction between commitment and sympathy, where commitment corresponds to our genuine altruism whilst sympathy covers those forms of altruism which may be accommodated within egoism.[30] Commitments are seen as motivators that are independent of utility, but commitments may be simultaneously directed towards a variety of ideals or groups. In this way, the individual may be thought of as incorporating a range of preference rankings each corresponding to a particular viewpoint or commitment. Furthermore, Sen argues for the possibility of a meta-ranking which ranks these various preference rankings according to the extent to which they articulate the individual's underlying moral beliefs. Thus, for example, an individual may be equipped with the subjective preferences of the standard egoist, a preference ranking reflecting the individual's commitment to each of, say, his local community, the environment and a political party, and a meta-ranking which allows him to answer questions concerning the relative moral worth of these various commitments in any particular situation.

The discussion of altruism within the framework provided by modelling an individual in terms of multiple preference rankings in exemplified by Margolis (1982) who adopts the simplified position in which the individual embodies just two rankings — one self-interested or egoist, the other group-interested or altruistic. Here we have a strong echo of the weakness of will problem (Section 2.4). In both cases the individual is conceived as being divided into two (or more) "actors" who would behave differently from each other. In the weakness of will case the separation is temporal whilst in the present setting the two commitments co-exist at a given time, but the inner struggle which is characteristic of the weakness of will problem carries over directly to the present case. In certain choice situations there will exist a tension between altruism and egoism which must be resolved internally. The analogy with weakness of will also indicates the possibility of the group-interested aspect of the individual binding or precommitting the self-interested aspect (or vice versa), perhaps by entering into long-term arrangements which reduce the opportunities for selfish (altruistic) actions in the future.

Extended rationality may, therefore, be defined in terms of the rejection of narrow self-interest as the sole motivator in favour of a view of rationality which recognises a number of distinct motivators or commitments (where self-interest may, of course, be included in that number). Such a view emphasises the internal tension between alternative commitments which may arise in certain circumstances and also allows a natural interpretation of the relevance of a conception of morality to rationality as a form of meta-ranking over alternative motivations.

2.6   UNCERTAINTY

The expected-utility-maximisation model of choice under uncertainty occupies a central position in the neoclassical view of rationality, and yet it is widely recognised that the predictions of the model are frequently and systematically violated.[31] This confrontation between the prevailing model of rational choice and the empirical evidence may produce any one of three reactions:

(1) The theoretical model as currently formulated is inaccurate in some details, but a "generalised" expected-utility model which fits the available evidence may exist which preserves the central characteristics of neoclassical rationality.
(2) The theoretical model remains an appropriate normative criterion of rationality, so that the empirical evidence indicates systematic irrationality, which requires subsidiary explanation.
(3) The theoretical model should be revised to provide a better description of behaviour even if this requires abandoning the neoclassical view of rationality.

Each of these lines of argument has been advanced in recent years and it is the intention of this section to review this debate in the light of the more general distinctions between neoclassical, imperfect and extended rationality. Of the three lines of argument noted, the first amounts to the reassertion of a neoclassical theory of perfect rationality, whilst the second advocates an imperfect rationality explanation of the observed deviations from full neoclassical rationality. The third argument then corresponds to an extended view of rationality in which the neoclassical approach is replaced by an alternative theory of perfect rationality.

Alongside this debate on the reform of uncertainty analysis there exists a more radical critique of the analysis associated with subjectivism, and I will offer an outline of this critique at the end of this section. But before discussing the debate it is necessary to be rather more precise about the content of the expected-utility-maximisation model in its standard form,[32] and the empirical evidence which casts doubt upon it.

The simplest statement of expected-utility theory begins with the requirement that the individual recognises that each feasible act carries with it an array of possible outcomes (pay-offs), each of which can be accurately evaluated in utility terms and associated with a subjective probability of occurrence. This array must be exhaustive in the sense that the subjective probabilities must sum to unity. The next step of the argument establishes that each act is evaluated as the weighted sum of the utilities of the possible pay-offs, where the relevant weights are simply the subjective probabilities. Thus the value, in utility terms, of an act is the expected value of its outcome. The final step of the argument then establishes that the rational individual will choose actions so as to maximise this expected utility value.

This argument can be shown to follow from a set of five simple axioms which can be informally stated as:

— Transitivity: the individual should have complete and transitive preferences over actions.
— Independence: if any two pay-offs are valued equally, then two lottery tickets which feature those pay-offs, and are in all other respects identical, must also be valued equally.
— Continuity: if three pay-offs are ranked X, Y, Z, then there is some lottery offering pay-offs X and Z which the individual will value as being equal to Y.
— Preference for high probability: if two lottery tickets offer the same two pay-offs but with different probabilities, an individual will prefer the lottery which offers the higher probability of the preferred pay-off.
— Compound probabilities: a two-stage lottery which offers a probability p of winning a probability q of winning pay-off X, will be valued equally with a single-stage lottery which offers a probability pq of winning pay-off X.

Empirical research into individual choice under uncertainty has thrown up a number of effects which contradict the expected-utility theory. Most basic amongst these effects are three which were restated and documented by Kahneman and Tversky (1979).

The "certainty" effect[33] is illustrated in Table 2.5. Individuals are first faced by the choice between A and B. Expected utility theory can tell us nothing about this individual choice, but a significant majority prefers the certainty of act B. The same individuals are now confronted with the choice between C and D. Again the theory cannot predict the outcome of this choice, but it does carry the implication that if B was preferred to A, then D should be preferred to C. However, in fact, C is preferred to D by a significant majority.

The "common consequence" effect[34] is illustrated in Table 2.6. Again, expected-utility theory cannot predict the choice between A and B or the choice between C and D, but it does imply that if B is preferred to A, then D must be preferred to C. However, this prediction is overturned empirically, with the significant majority preferring B to A and C to D.

The "isolation" effect[35] concerns uncertainty decomposed into two stages and is illustrated in Table 2.7. Here the choice between A and B is a simple one-stage gamble whilst the choice between C and D involves two stages. Expected-utility theory then implies that if A is preferred to B, C must be preferred to D. Once again, the empirical evidence

Table 2.5: The Certainty Effect

Act	Pay-offs	Probabilities
A	4000/0	0.8/0.2
B	3000	1
C	4000/0	0.2/0.8
D	3000/0	0.25/0.75

Table 2.6: The Common Consequence Effect

Act	Pay-offs	Probabilities
A	2500/2400/0	0.33/0.66/0.01
B	2400	1
C	2500/0	0.33/0.67
D	2400/0	0.34/0.66

Table 2.7: The Isolation Effect

Act	Pay-offs	Probabilities
A	4000/0	0.2/0.8
B	3000/0	0.25/0.75
C	E/0	0.25/0.75
D	F/0	0.25/0.75
E	4000/0	0.8/0.2
F	3000	1

rejects this implication with the significant majority preferring A to B and D to C.

These three effects, and others like them, illustrate the apparently irrational behaviour of individuals faced with well-specified choices under uncertainty. Since the demonstration of these effects is couched in terms of the inconsistency of choices, it is natural to think first of a breakdown of means-rationality as the underlying source of the difficulties but, as we shall see, each of the three approaches to the reform of the analysis identified above can make some progress towards providing an explanation of observed behaviour.

This first reaction to these empirical observations attempts to reassert the neoclassical view of rationality, and is exemplified by Machina (1982) whose strategy is to relax the independence axiom which effectively insists that the individual's preferences must be linear in the probabilities, and replace it with a less restrictive assumption which merely insists that preferences vary smoothly with the probabilities.[36] This strategy allows Machina to develop a "generalised expected utility analysis" which maintains neoclassical means-rationality (ie choice is fully consistent and transitive since the transitivity axiom is still enforced), and retains the maximisation of personal (expected) utility as the sole motivator of action, whilst extending the range of observed behaviour consistent with the theory. In fact both the certainty effect and the common consequence effect outlined above are consistent with Machina's generalised theory.[37]

However, the isolation effect is not consistent with the generalised neoclassical theory, so the project cannot be judged a complete success. Nevertheless, the fundamental point is that it may be possible, by detailed analysis, to generalise the theory further in a manner which does not weaken the normative claim of neoclassical rationality and yet which renders observed behaviour consistent with that notion of rationality.

The second reaction to the empirical evidence may be exemplified by Kahneman and Tversky (1979) themselves who do not challenge the normative basis of neoclassical rationality, but offer a theory of imperfectly rational decision-making under uncertainty which is designed to incorporate the variety of apparent failings of rationality revealed empirically. Thus, for example, individuals are argued to "round" probability values in a way which would account directly for the choice of C over D in Table 2.6 above (if 0.33 and 0.34 are perceived as the same, C is clearly the "rational" choice). This procedure essentially provides a descriptive theory by hypothesising about the nature of individuals' perceptions, and can be likened to the bounded-rationality approach (Section 2.4) in that it is failings of perception and judgement which explain the departures from fully rational behaviour.

If this line of argument is accepted, one might expect misperception to be dispelled by the direct provision of accurate information. But the evidence on this point is rather mixed. It is certainly the case that some individuals who originally make "irrational" choices reverse their decisions when the situation is fully explained; but it seems that many individuals persist with their original choice even when they fully understand the implications.[38] This must be taken as casting some doubt upon the imperfect rationality argument as a total explanation of the original choices.

The third reaction is exemplified by Loomes and Sugden (1982) who attempt to provide a theory of choice under uncertainty which effectively challenges the neoclassical view of rationality at the normative level whilst improving on its ability to explain observed behaviour at the descriptive level. Their approach is based on the extended-rationality strategy of introducing the notion of regret as a motivator of action alongside (expected) utility. Regret, in this setting, is experienced in a way that depends upon the set of actions that were available to the individual. Thus, if action X is chosen and Y rejected, the utility pay-off depends only on the action X and the state of the world which is revealed when the uncertainty is resolved. However, regret (or its converse, rejoicing) will depend not only upon the utility pay-off of action X but also on the pay-off that would have accrued in that particular state of the world if action Y had been chosen. Once regret of this form is accepted, Loomes and Sugden argue that it is entirely reasonable for the individual to anticipate regret and take account of it in making the original decision. The individual is then argued to maximise "modified expected utility."

This approach is relatively successful in providing a theoretical basis for much of the empirical work. Indeed each of the three effects discussed above is fully consistent with the extended theory although some empirical observations are still unexplained. But perhaps the most interesting aspect of the theory is that, in terms of the axiomatic structure of expected-utility theory, it is the axiom of transitivity which is abandoned.[39] This intransitivity of choice under the extended theory clearly contrasts with the neoclassical notion of means-rationality, just as the introduction of a motivator other than utility contrasts with the notion of ends-rationality.

As in the case of altruism (Section 2.5) it could be argued that the "anticipation of regret" and "regret" contribute to utility rather than complement it; so that the "modified utility function" could be reinterpreted as a simple utility function and utility-maximisation reinstated by the back door. But this argument is not persuasive. Even if the relabelling of the modified utility function were allowed, "utility" would still depend upon the rejected actions as well as the chosen action, and it is this dependence which provides the intransitivity of choice. In this way it is not possible to reinterpret the model as utility-maximisation (in the first sense discussed in Section 2.2) since the associated choices will not be consistent in the relevant sense. More fundamentally, it can be argued that even the relabelling of the modified utility function is illicit since regret is distinct from utility (though dependent on it) in way that requires a separate treatment in the analysis of decision-making under uncertainty.

Which of the three reactions to the contrast between the standard view of rationality under uncertainty and the observed behaviour offers the best way forward? The second approach offers a purely descriptive model of choice which focusses on misperception and misjudgement. It is difficult to deny that such mistakes are common in practice, so that the model of imperfect rationality has a real role to play. However, it seems unreasonable to attempt to explain all of the peculiarities of observed behaviour in this way. It would therefore seem attractive to embed this theory of imperfect rationality within one or other of the models of perfectly rational choice under uncertainty which form the first and third approaches.

Each of the first and third approaches offers a generalisation of the standard view, but along very different lines. Each can be seen as successful in extending the range of empirical prediction, and each has considerable intuitive or introspective support. The choice between these approaches depends, as always, on the purpose of the choice. If descriptive accuracy is all that is required then each has its relative merits depending upon the precise types of behaviour to be modelled. But if choice between the models is to be made at the normative level then the real question is whether the line of argument exemplified by Loomes and Sugden is psychologically coherent. If regret is a genuine sensation distinct from utility, then it is difficult to deny its potential relevance to decision-making, whatever implications this may carry at the descriptive level.

Whilst this three-cornered debate on choice under uncertainty is illustrative of the deeper debate on rationality identified in previous sections, there is a fourth position — the subjectivist position — which offers a more radical critique of the neoclassical view. In the present context it is not possible to do more than offer a very brief sketch of the subjectivist critique of choice under uncertainty which will be of direct use in our later discussion (Section 3.5).[40]

In its most radical form, the subjectivist position argues that each choice-situation is a unique and unrepeatable experience which cannot be fully understood in terms of general models. Of course this does not deny that general models may be of considerable value (eg in describing the regularities of aggregate behaviour) but these models are seen as purely conventional by the subjectivist since they fail to capture the essence of the situation being modelled.

In the area of uncertainty the neoclassical model is, to a degree, subjectivist, since it recognises that subjective probabilities inform the individual's expected-utility calculus, but full subjectivism would go much further than this. The modelling of uncertainty as a well-defined, albeit subjective, probability distribution over an exhaustive list of possible outcomes is rejected by the subjectivist, who argues for an interpretation of uncertainty as the unknowable rather than the merely probabilistic. Once this position is accepted, it is clearly impossible to reconstruct any theory of choice which depends upon a maximisation of expected utility.

Compare this with the imperfectly rational view of Kahneman and Tversky (1979) where misperception was advanced as the major source of failure of the neoclassical model. Subjectivists would certainly accept that misperception plays an important role in decision-making, but they would cut the notion of imperfect rationality free from its connection with perfect neoclassical rationality. The subjectivist would not accept the perfect model as a relevant criterion so that he is not in a position to recognise his own irrationality and attempt to improve upon it. Rather he is set in a context of profound uncertainty without the benefit of any external criteria, and he simply makes choices.

In viewing choice, the subjectivist wishes to emphasise the contextual and perceptual characteristics of the choice situation and thereby understand the process by which individuals translate the fragmented and incomplete information available to them into action. There are many similarities here with the bounded-rationality argument of Simon, but again the subjectivist takes the idea one step further by dispensing with the external criterion of perfect rationality.

The belief-model of the full subjectivist is radically different from that labelled subjective belief-rational in our earlier discussion (Section 2.2). That label was used to indicate an individual with a complete but objectively false model of the world. Radical subjectivism is not concerned with such an individual who (falsely) believes he knows everything (or, at least, the probability of everything). If such an individual ever existed, subjectivists would claim that no real decision-making need ever occur — all that is required is mechanical calculation. By contrast, the fully subjectivist individual does not have a specified or complete model at all; he knows that he is ignorant, but not precisely what he is ignorant of, nor can he list the possible consequences of any action, still less attach probabilities to them. To such an individual, the external criterion of neoclassical rationality (or any other theory of perfect rationality) is simply incoherent; "rational action" to such a person can mean no more than "reasonable action" — any action which can be suggested by the application of limited reason to the available information in the particular context.

The subjectivist critique may be seen as encompassing the positions associated with both imperfect and extended rationality. I have already indicated the possibility of interpreting subjectivism as a generalisation of imperfect rationality, and it is equally possible to cast subjectivism as a generalisation of extended rationality. Take, for example, the notion of regret discussed by Loomes and Sugden. To the subjectivist, regret is simply one aspect of the complex internal mechanism by which an individual attempts to learn from the mistakes which he will inevitably make. This mechanism, which will involve the ex-post reappraisal of decisions made in the attempt to improve the "reasonableness" of future decisions, is, however, not itself capable of complete anticipation. Thus, whilst the subjectivist would certainly applaud the introduction of regret into the model of decision-making, he would be sceptical of the idea of perfectly anticipated regret, and he would also doubt the wisdom of focussing on the particular notion of regret rather than the more general notion of an imperfect learning mechanism.

Despite this ability to subsume imperfect and extended rationality within a more general, if rather vague, subjectivism, it will be convenient in most of what follows to retain the distinction between imperfect and extended theories of rationality so as to be able to view their separate implications.

2.7   RULES, RIGHTS AND OBLIGATION

Having developed and compared the major positions in the debate on rationality, it is the task of this section to bring these various ideas together to provide a preliminary discussion of a topic which will be of considerable importance to our later analysis of social institutions. This topic is the nature of the rational reaction to the existence of the institutional rules and rights which form the state.

As a preliminary, these institutional rules and rights must be distinguished from both internal rules and moral rights. Internal rules of the type associated with procedural rationality and strategies of precommitment are strictly intrapersonal devices which are designed to restructure the internal decision-making process. They are imposed by an individual on himself. Institutional rules, on the other hand, are essentially inter-personal or social devices which set out to influence behaviour in the pursuit of some conception of a collective goal. Such rules are imposed from outside the individual.

The distinction between institutional and moral rights depends upon the distinction between empirical and ethical support. An institutional right is one which is as a matter of fact, embodied within a particular society; whilst a moral right can be identified only by appeal to a particular theory of ethics. Moral rights are independent of institutional rights, whilst institutional rights may depend upon moral rights for their justification.[41]

Institutional rules and rights of the type that concern us here may take either one of two forms: *laws* which are enforced within society so that non-compliance will typically involve a coercive penalty, and *norms* which embody socially accepted behaviour patterns which are not externally enforced. Norms must be seen as essentially self-enforcing.[42]

Norms, by their definition, conform with individually rational behaviour. Any particular theory of rationality will, therefore, generate a particular view of the range of norms which may be expected to emerge. This line of enquiry will be taken up in some detail in Chapter 4.

Laws, by contrast, appear to operate in tension with individually rational behaviour. It is this tension, and its interpretation across alternative views of rationality, that requires further discussion here. We may begin with the neoclassical theory of rationality and its analysis of the individually rational response to institutional laws.

The neoclassical view of rationality can accept no duty or obligation upon the individual to respect the law *qua* law. On the contrary, the law *per se* will have no direct influence on individual decision-making. However, the threats of punishment which enforce the law will influence behaviour by making illegal actions more costly. Thus the neoclassically rational individual reacts to the threat of punishment rather than the law itself, so that we may model the law in terms of changing the relative prices of alternative actions rather than placing any new constraints on acceptable behaviour.

In this way the neoclassical theory of rationality denies the Hohfeldian relationship between rights and obligations.[43] A legal right does not, in this view, carry with it any obligation to respect that right. Notice that this point concerning the absence of obligation in the neoclassical theory does not depend upon any particular view of the origin or justification of the law. An example may clarify this assertion. Suppose that the process of law-making in a particular society involves the requirement of unanimous consent. Even in this extreme case where each law is the outcome of direct and voluntary agreement, it is still the case that a strictly neoclassically rational individual who was a party to the original agreement has no special reason to respect the law.

I may value the law — and so vote for it — if my expectation of that law's overall impact on my welfare (largely deriving from my belief that *you* may obey the law) is positive. However, I may simultaneously decide to break that law in a particular case if the private benefit exceeds the threatened punishment.

As we have seen, free-riding of this sort is a common companion of the neoclassical theory of rationality. In this instance the difficulty arises from the fact that prior agreement is not in itself a binding precommitment since, like the law itself, prior agreement fails to impose any obligation on the strictly neoclassical man.

So far we have been concerned with the neoclassical man's direct reaction to the law as it attempts to constrain or otherwise influence his behaviour. Two further aspects of the rational response to law require some comment. The first concerns the situation in which an individual is able to provide a third-party defence of the law at some cost to himself. Here the central tenet of egoism indicates that the neoclassical man will not defend the law, or the legal rights of others, unless there is an expectation of personal reward which exceeds the direct costs. This reward may be direct and obvious, or more subtle as in the case of the expected value of a reputation, or the expectation of induced reciprocal action by others; but in any event there can be no obligation acting on the individual to provide third-party defence.

The final point concerns the rational action of an individual holder of a legal right. Here a neoclassical rights holder will always use his right to gain maximum advantage for himself. Of course, this may involve an individual in waiving a particular right in a particular situation in order to gain a greater advantage in the long run. But such actions must be understood in the same light as the self-interested altruism discussed in Section 2.5. The neoclassically rational man could never waive a right, or release someone from a legal debt, out of any motive other than long-run self-interest.

In summary, then, the neoclassical theory of rationality denies the possibilitty of any individualistic concept of duty or obligation, so that legal rules and rights simply enter the individuals' decision-making calculus as alterations in the relative prices of alternative actions.

Whatever theory of rationality is accepted, it is unlikely that respect for legal rights, or for the law more generally, can be absolute. The standard economic analysis deriving from the neoclassical viewpoint takes the extreme position that such respect is entirely absent and that obedience to the law is wholly contingent upon the calculation of self-interest. But any theory of rationality which preserves individual autonomy must regard respect for the law as being contingent, to at least some degree, upon some further consideration. To illustrate this we may now turn to the question of the status of legal rules and rights, and the possibility of obligation, in the imperfect and extended views of rationality.

The imperfect rationality school of thought suggests a strong parallel between external institutional rules and the internal rules of precommitment. Thus the law, or even a weaker norm, might form a convenient external "signpost" for an imperfectly rational individual to adopt as a standard of personal behaviour. In this way the imperfectly rational individual may precommit himself to a law-abiding strategy as a general, and low-cost, means of improving his rationality.

Of course, as we have already seen (Section 2.4) such imperfectly rational precommitment cannot be fully binding on the individual. Whilst the individual may owe an obligation to himself in respect of his adoption of the law-abiding strategy, this obligation is not overwhelming since it acts only to tip the scale in favour of respect for the law in cases where self-interest does not obviously indicate a course of action. In particular cases where breaking the law is clearly in the individual's self-interest, the obligation to abide by the law simply vanishes. This form of obligation grants the law the benefit of any doubt. This may not seem like a particularly strong force in favour of law-abiding behaviour; but in the imperfectly rational world doubt is of the essence.

The extended rationality school of thought would also stress the possibility of interpreting institutional rules and rights as the external artifacts of individual strategies of precommitment, but the details of this interpretation differ considerably from the details of the imperfectly rational view.

Precommitment, to the individual characterised by extended rationality, is a matter of the establishment of a binding constraint which promotes one commitment over another (Section 2.5). Such precommitment is advantageous only to the extent that it is binding, and to the extent that it originates from the meta-preferences of the individual, rather than from the doubt which surrounds the imperfectly rational individual.

In this way we can see that an individual who precommits himself out of extended rationality to abide by a particular law does so precisely to *constrain* himself and not simply to *influence* his own behaviour. The meta-preference is the source of obligation here and it implies a full respect for particular laws, but it does not necessarily extend to an obligation to respect all laws *qua* laws.

Where imperfect rationality may generate a weak obligation to abide by the law in general, extended rationality is to be conceived as generating a strong obligation to abide by particular laws which are seen by the individual as promoting his meta-preferences despite a tension between the law and self-interest in its narrow interpretation.

In both cases the source of obligation lies within the individual rather than being derived directly from the existence of the law itself. Obligation and legal rights or laws are independently generated in this view and take on the Hohfeldian relationship only in very special circumstances.

The major distinction between these views of institutional rules and rights and the neoclassical view is twofold. First, the alternative views grant some place for obligation in the discussion of rational behaviour and so place some weight on rules *qua* rules, rather than relying entirely on appeals to calculations of self-interest via long-run arguments or the notion of deterrence. Self-interest and deterrence clearly have a role to play in the analysis, but their role is limited once a form of obligation can be grounded in rationality.

Second, and more fundamentally, the alternative views suggest very different approachs to the linkages between the individual and the state, and the process of derivation of institutional rules. Under the neoclassical view, laws are the domain of external authority — the state. Such a state and its laws may be popular in the sense that individuals may recognise them to be of positive value, but this value is derived from the state's ability to coerce and constrain others. At the personal level, the state must be seen as interfering and restrictive. Similarly, the state may be democratic in the sense that it responds to individual opinion via some procedure, but to any individual the state must seem beyond control since it is necessary for the laws which structure and transform social situations to be seen as exogenous changes in relative prices by all individuals.

Compare this to the situation under either alternative view of individual rationality. Here any individual may see the law — or at least some laws — as personally beneficial not simply because of its restrictive effect on others, but also because of its direct effects on him. Equally, the individual can easily recognise the endogeneity of the law-making process as an area in which he can enter into a range of external precommitments, subject to the desire for such precommitments being widespread.

This discussion clearly brings us close to the central topic of this book and provides a number of hints as to how our discussion of rationality will be of value in viewing the institutions of state. All of these hints will be followed up in Chapter 4.

2.8   INTERIM CONCLUSIONS

The bulk of this chapter has been devoted to the criticism of the neoclassical theory of rationality and the establishment, at least in outline form, of alternative views of individual rationality. The recent growth in the volume of criticism of the mainstream neoclassical viewpoint, and the variety of sources of such criticism — both within economics and in related disciplines — suggests a developing dissatisfaction with the basic neoclassical view, at least when it is used in attempts to model general social interaction. However, it would be entirely wrong to suggest that the neoclassical view is anything less than the dominant approach. Both within economics and elsewhere in social science, reference to the "rational choice model" always carries the implication of neoclassical rationality.

We can identify four interrelated themes which stand out from our various lines of argument. The idea of inherent limitations on individuals, and the recognition of — and reaction to — such limitations form the first theme and also provide one motivation for strategies of precommitment which form the second theme. However not all precommitments derive from second-best or rationality-improving strategies. This provides the distinction between non-binding precommitments which do arise in this manner, and binding precommitments which relate more directly to our third theme — that of the existence of motivators or commitments other than self-interest. This notion, and the related ideas of meta-preferences and the provision of a personal basis for morality, also links into our fourth theme — that of the recognition of an inner-struggle of rationality played out within the individual.

In the context of meta-preferences, this inner struggle is best thought of as a tension between alternative and potentially competing commitments; but the idea of an inner struggle also relates back directly to our first theme — that of inherent limitations. Here the inner struggle is simply a struggle against irrationality, with rationality seen as a valued but unattainable prize rather than as a definitional property of human choice.

Each of the imperfect and extended views of rationality outlined and illustrated in the preceding sections contains these themes in varying proportions. Whilst the two viewpoints are strictly independent of each other, they are certainly compatible. Indeed, I have already suggested that it is possible to combine them within the radically subjectivist position.

The imperfect theory of rationality can only fully define itself relative to a specified theory of perfect rationality. We may, therefore, use the distinctions made in this chapter to identify four classes of theories. The perfect neoclassical theory of rationality which has acted as our starting point forms the first of these and is a class with only one member. Imperfect neoclassical theories form the second class, which includes all those theories which accept the perfect neoclassical view as the target of each individual's struggle against inherent limitations of any sort.

The third class contains all extended theories of rationality which carry self-interest theory within them as one of the individualistic commitments, but which differ from each other in terms of which other commitments are recognised. Finally, we have the class of imperfect-extended theories which contains those views which combine all of the criticisms of the perfect neoclassical model discussed here in offering views of rationality as an imperfect striving for some extended vision of perfect rationality.

Each of these four classes of theory carries with it implications for the tension between individual rationality and any particular ethic. These tensions and the possibility of their institutional accommodation form the subject matter of Chapter 4. However, before we can begin that discussion we must first consider in more detail the nature of the ethic which provides the second force in generating the tension. This is the task of Chapter 3.

3 Ethics

3.1 FIVE VIEWS OF ETHICS

Theories of ethics are concerned ultimately with the comparative evaluation of alternative social states and, therefore, with the criteria which are to be used in evaluating social change. The range of ethical theories, and variants within theories, is enormous and no attempt will be made to survey even the contemporary literature.[1] Rather, I will simply advance five views of ethics which are currently influential, so as to be able to discuss their relative strengths and weaknesses and, eventually, to be able to compare their implications regarding the theory of the state and its relationship with the individual.

Ethical theories may take any one of a number of forms. One obvious distinction is that between substantive theories, which are directly concerned with identifying the nature of the social good, and procedural theories, which are views about the way in which a substantive concept of the social good may emerge. Within the class of substantive theories we may further distinguish between end-state principles of social good which argue that it is possible to evaluate the goodness of a social situation at a moment in time solely on the basis of evidence concerning that moment in time, and historical principles which argue that the evaluation of a situation will in general depend upon how the situation has arisen. Of course, these two distinctions give rise to four possible structures (substantive/end-state, substantive/historical, procedural/end-state and procedural/historical) and the five theories of ethics to be discussed will include representatives of each of these possibilities.

A further common distinction is that between ethical theories which are based on some particular view of individual ends, and those which are formally independent of such ends. This distinction clearly relates back to our earlier discussion of individualistic ends-rationality, but again the five selected views of ethics cover both positions.

A final distinction worthy of note at this stage concerns the range of ethically admissible evidence allowed by any particular theory. On the one hand there are the individualistic theories which argue that individuals are and must be the only source of ethical value so that, for example, if one situation is better than another, it must be better for someone. On the other hand, non-individualistic theories view individuals as just one amongst several possible sources of ethical value, so that impersonal entities — such as a group of individuals — may be sources of value over and above any purely individualistic value. Under such theories it would be quite meaningful for one situation to be declared better than another even though it was better for no one. Both sides of this distinction are also represented within our five chosen views of ethics.

The first of the views to be discussed is utilitarianism, which has for so long been the dominant tradition within economics and elsewhere in the social sciences and still forms the theory against which all other theories are most obviously contrasted. In terms of the categories outlined above, utilitarianism is a substantive, end-state theory that is dependent upon a particular view of individual ends and is individualistic in nature.

Paretianism, the second view to be discussed, is perhaps less widely regarded as a theory of ethics than any of the other four. Nevertheless, the Pareto criterion is widely used within mainstream economics, where it is often portrayed as a minimalist value judgement, and so it deserves attention in our present context. As is widely recognised, Paretianism is a particularly restricted form of utilitarianism and so carries some of the same characteristics as its parent, although the precise formulation and implications of Paretianism are importantly distinct from those of utilitarianism.

Like utilitarianism our third view of ethics, liberalism, exists in a wide variety of forms and is often linked with economics. I shall make some attempt at distinguishing between a number of strains of contemporary liberalism but I shall concentrate attention on the libertarian liberalism which has been in the ascendancy in recent years. On the classificatory scheme outlined above, most versions of liberalism are substantive, historical theories which are independent of individual ends but are none the less individualistic.

Contractarianism, the fourth view to be considered, differs from the three preceding views primarily because it is a procedural theory. This being so, it is clear that the substantive view of ethics which may emerge from a contractarian procedure is of somewhat secondary significance to the principal thrust of the theory. Nevertheless, a range of alternative substantive views have recently been derived from contractarian premises, and we shall briefly review these as well as focussing more carefully on the procedural aspect of contractarianism. The substantive view of ethics deriving from contractarianism may be either end-state or historical, dependent upon or independent of individual ends, and either individualistic or not. Indeed, I shall argue that the contractarian procedural position, though not without its weaknesses, provides a useful device for gaining a degree of comparability between alternative ethical theories.

The fifth and final viewpoint to be discussed is that associated with recent developments in the Marxian tradition. Marx's own ethical theory is a matter of considerable and continuing controversy, but we shall view a current interpretation of Marxian theory as it relates to the evaluation of social situations. This interpretation is substantive, historical, independent of individual ends and broadly non-individualistic.

In each of the discussions to be presented in the next five sections, the purpose is simply to outline the fundamental nature of the ethical view and to expose some of the major contemporary lines of argument advanced in favour of, or against, any particular view. There is no intention to offer anything resembling a historical review of the development of each theory, nor anything resembling an accurate charting of the full range of sub-positions which exist within each theory.

Once each of the five views has been established, Section 3.7 turns to the topic of comparative discussion. This discussion will be centred around the various treatments of a number of issues central to any ethical theory. The intention of this discussion is to stress similarities amongst the various theories reviewed and to suggest the possibility of a form of procedural meta-ethic which will be of value in our later discussion of the state, and which relates back to our discussions of individual rationality.

3.2   UTILITARIANISM

Classic utilitarianism[2] can be separated into three basic parts. Following Sen and Williams (1982) we may name these parts welfarism, sum-ranking and consequentialism. Welfarism[3] is the view that individual welfare levels or utilities are the only legitimate basis for the assignment of ethical value. Welfarism is, therefore, responsible for reducing the stock of ethically relevant information contained in a social situation to a vector of utility levels with one element for each individual.

The sum-ranking component of utilitarianism then asserts that the appropriate means for establishing the precise value to be assigned to a social situation is simply the addition of the elements of the utility vector. Thus, sum-ranking ensures that the ethical value of a situation is simply the sum of the utilities of the individuals who make up that situation.

Finally, consequentialism provides the prescriptive element of utilitarianism by asserting that choices regarding actions which affect or determine social situations should be made solely by reference to the ethical value of the social state which arises as a consequence of the action. From a mutually exclusive set of possibilities that action which maximises consequent utility is to be chosen.

There are many variants of the argument for utilitarianism,[4] but I wish to focus on just two, one of which grounds utilitarianism in the judgement of an idealised and impartial observer of society, whilst the other grounds it directly in individually rational choice.

The impartial observer argument effectively personalises the ethical problem by setting a neutral and sympathetic observer as judge over alternative social states and enquiring as to the principles he might use to reach his judgement.[5] Impartiality in this context implies that the observer must show equal concern for each individual and, therefore, equal respect for the preferences of each individual. As Rawls notes:

Endowed with ideal powers of sympathy and imagination, the impartial spectator is the perfectly rational individual who identifies with and experiences the desires of others as if these desires were his own. In this way he ascertains the intensity of these desires and assigns them their appropriate weight in the one system of desire the satisfaction of which the ideal legislator then tries to maximise by adjusting the rules of the social system. (Rawls, 1971 p. 27).

Utilitarianism follows directly from this consideration of the impartial observer given the elevation of desires to ethical status (welfarism), the presumption of neoclassical rationality (consequentialism) and the equal treatment of individuals (sum-ranking).

In criticism of this argument, Rawls points out that:

This view of social cooperation is the consequence of extending to society the principles of choice for one man, and then, to make this extension work, conflating all persons into one through the imaginative acts of the impartial sympathetic spectator. Utilitarianism does not take seriously the distinction between persons. (Rawls, 1971, p. 27)

Thus, the major criticism of the impartial observer argument for utilitarianism focuses on the inappropriateness of the analogy between individual choice and the choice of an essentially social ethic, and so points to the distinction between persons as an ethically relevant consideration which is overlooked by utilitarianism.

The second argument for utilitarianism derives from the formal additivity properties of utility functions.[6] The same logic which argues that an individual's utility function when facing uncertain outcomes is the (weighted) sum of the utilities under each possible outcome, can be employed to show that utility functions can be summed across individuals to provide an aggregate measure of social utility. Harsanyi suggests that this is so for the normal interpretation of a utility function which simply represents an individual's own conception of his own interests.[7] This argument then gives rise to classic utilitarianism. Broome (1983), on the other hand, uses "utility function" in a much wider sense to identify what is actually good for the individual — regardless of his own conception of his interest.[8] This allows Broome's version of utilitarianism to escape any criticism directed at welfarism, at the cost of leaving undefined what is good for an individual.

Whichever interpretation of "utility" is adopted, utilitarianism (ie sum-ranking and consequentialism) results from the particular form of additivity and, as Broome points out, this requires that utility (in whichever interpretation) must be additive in all dimensions and not just across individuals and uncertain outcomes. The particular dimension Broome focusses on is additivity across the stages of an individual's life, where he presents the following example.[9] An individual faces two possible lives, each of two periods duration; the utility that he will enjoy in each period of each possible life is uncertain as indicated in Table 3.1.

Each life provides an expectation of 3 units of utility in total. Life 1 ensures this total but indicates uncertainty over the timing of utility flows. Life 2 provides a certainty that the two periods will be equally good but an uncertainty as to the total lifetime utility, which may be either 4 or 2. The form of additivity required by utilitarianism then requires that these two lives be equally valued; the two lives are equally good in each period (each offers a 50/50 chance of either one or two units of utility) and so must be equally

Table 3.1: Additive Utility

		Utility	
	Probability	Period 1	Period 2
Life 1	0.5	2	1
	0.5	1	2
Life 2	0.5	2	2
	0.5	1	1

good overall. But this is by no means obviously true. If Life 1 is preferred to Life 2 (or vice versa) utilitarianism is false.

Each of these lines of argument for utilitarianism has its potential counter. The impersonal observer argument is countered by the claim that utilitarianism "conflates all persons into one" and so ignores the ethically relevant distinction between people. The additivity argument is confronted with a plausible counter-example which, if accepted, denies utilitarianism. Having viewed these general lines of argument we now turn to the three identified component parts of utilitarianism to review briefly the debate on each.

Welfarism can be discussed in the context of another simple example, this one deriving from Sen (1979a). Table 3.2 shows the utility levels of each of two individuals in each of three social states.

Welfarism implies that states y and z *must* be valued equally since, in utility terms, they are identical. Sen's

Table 3.2: Welfarism

	Social State		
	x	y	z
1's Utility	4	7	7
2's Utility	10	8	8

demonstration of the limitations of welfarism consists of supplying further information about the social states:

In x person 1 is hungry while 2 is eating a great deal. In y person 2 has been made to surrender a part of his food supply to 1 . . . . Consider now z. Here person 1 is still as hungry as in x, and person 2 is also eating just as much. However, person 1, who is a sadist, is now permitted to torture 2, who — alas — is not a masochist. (Sen, 1979a, pp. 547–8)

To the welfarist, this additional information must be irrelevant. The *only* ethically relevant facts are the utility levels, however they have come about. If we wish to take the new information into account in judging between y and z, or in ranking them relative to x, we must be in breach of welfarism.

This example illustrates the fact that welfarism is a particularly restrictive version of the principle of end-state evaluation. Sen's example, suitably adapted, could be used as a critique of any purely end-state ethical criteria. We have already noted Broome's avoidance of welfarism by making some wider conception of the good the relevant ethical information rather than common utility. In reply to Sen's example, Broome could simply observe that if sadism (or compulsory food transfers) is held to be bad then this judgement would be reflected in the broader measure of utility which could be generated for each of the social states. Broome's point is then that ethics can be broken down into two questions — what is good for an individual, and how the good should be aggregated. Utilitarianism (ie sum-ranking) may be a contender as an answer to the second question, but it provides no answer to the first if welfarism is rejected.

The sum-ranking component of utilitarianism has already been seen to imply that the distinction between individuals in treated as ethically unimportant. As Hammond notes in a slightly different context:

Individuals are no more than the pieces in a utilitarian game, to be manipulated for utilitarian ends, though with their best interest in mind. (Hammond, 1982, p. 101)

Any attempt to reintroduce concern for individuals *qua* individuals must breach sum-ranking. One tempting possibility here is to define an aggregate utility function with the individual utilities as arguments, but without imposing the sum-ranking restriction. Although such a function allows differential treatment of different individuals (and therefore runs counter to the impartial observer argument for utilitarianism), it is difficult to see how it demonstrates concern for individuals *qua* individuals. The shift from simple addition to weighted addition or some more complex form of aggregation still leaves the individual as a mere means of "producing" additional aggregate utility. It is one of the ironies of utilitarianism, and the social welfare function generalisation of utilitarianism, that whilst the theory is individualistic in the sense that only individuals count, it is wholly anti-individualistic in the sense that individuals are viewed as means.

Welfarism and sum-ranking, taken together, imply that all ethically relevant values are commensurable, that all values share a common yardstick.[10] As we have seen in Chapter 2, commensurability at the individualistic level is a basic property of the neoclassical approach to rationality. Any challenge to commensurability at this level must be grounded in an alternative theory of rationality. At the social level, commensurability amounts to the ability to aggregate utilities (or other values) across individuals.[11] We have already raised some issues in this area in discussing the sum-ranking component of utilitarianism. The rejection of commensurability at this level is a major feature of Paretianism, to be discussed in the next section. The general topic of commensurability will also be raised again in later sections.

The consequentialist aspect of utilitarianism has been discussed in the context of the appropriate utilitarian policy advice in situations of uncertainty. A much discussed example is provided by Diamond (1967). A policy (A or B) must be chosen before the uncertainty concerning which of two social states (x or y) will occur is resolved. The various possible utility consequences for the two individuals concerned are shown in Table 3.3.[12]

Table 3.3: Uncertainty and Utilitarianism

Policy	A		B	
Social State	x	y	x	y
1's Utility	1	1	1	0
2's Utility	0	0	0	1

From a strictly utilitarian perspective the choice between policies is a matter of indifference since each policy generates an identical ex-post utility level in both states. However, Diamond argues that policy B may be strictly preferred since it offers both individuals "a fair shake" in the sense that their ex-ante expected utilities will be equal even though their ex-post actual utilities will not.

That Diamond's claim is anti-utilitarian is clear, but precisely which component of utilitarianism is under criticism is somewhat less clear. One interpretation would suggest that sum-ranking is the source of the problem since it is the distribution of expected utilities across individuals which is claimed to be of ethical significance. On the other hand Broome (1983b) has argued that Diamond's criticism is based on the intrinsic valuation of fairness. This then would suggest a breach of welfarism, and could be overcome if fairness was included in a broader conception of the good which was then taken to be the input to a utilitarian aggregation procedure. However, Diamond's claim is also open to an anti-consequentialist interpretation since it emphasises the point that aspects of a policy other than its final consequences may be of importance in choosing amongst policies.

The distinction between ex-ante and ex-post utility levels, and its implications for social decision-making, has been discussed at considerable length since Diamond's contribution.[13] The simple point to note here is that the introduction of uncertainty opens the door to a line of criticism of utilitarianism essentially similar to that discussed in the context of additivity across the stages of an individual's life (Table 3.1 above). Once certainty over outcomes or their distribution may be valued independently of utility outcomes themselves, a departure from classic utilitarianism seems assured.

As before, the strategy of including the value of certainty/distribution in a expanded definition of utility is a perfectly acceptable way of reinstating sum-ranking as a possible aggregation technique, but it sacrifices the foundation of utilitarianism in actual individual (rational) behaviour. Furthermore, the individualism of utilitarianism is in some doubt if concepts of the good other than those actually held by the individuals in question have to be employed. The standard response to this doubt is to argue that the broader concept of utility is the conception that the individual would have if he were fully informed, fully rational, and so on. However, our earlier discussion of rationality suggests the difficulty of identifying such a perfectly prudent conception of an individual's interests, and this difficulty would carry over directly to the utilitarian context.

In summary then, if welfarism is accepted, utilitarianism has a relatively firm basis in individualism, but the arguments in favour of sum-ranking and consequentialism are by no means obviously persuasive. These arguments can be improved somewhat if welfarism is rejected, but this weakens the substance of utilitarianism in order to strengthen its claim as a simple method of aggregation, and also leaves utilitarianism without a clear basis in individualism.

3.3 PARETIANISM

Paretianism has a special relationship with utilitarianism whilst being distinguished from it principally by the refusal to adopt the sum-ranking characteristic, or indeed *any* method of aggregating individual utilities. Paretianism in its strongest form accepts welfarism and consequentialism but responds to the criticism which condemns utilitarianism for ignoring the distinction between individuals by maintaining the complete ethical independence of each individual. The impossibility of inter-personal comparisons of utility and, therefore, the impossibility of defining any aggregation procedure, is the hallmark of the Paretian position, which forms the basis of much formal welfare economic analysis.[14]

On the basis of this strong individualism the full Pareto criterion declares a social state A to be superior to state B if and only if at least one individual prefers A to B whilst no individuals prefer B to A. Each individual has an effective veto.

The apparent limitation of this criterion as an ethical stance is its ability to make comparisons between states where there is no unanimity either way. There is no implication that such incomparable states are equally valued. The Paretian view provides only a partial ordering over states and it has often been suggested that this in itself renders Paretianism unacceptable as a full ethical theory, although it is by no means obvious why an ethical theory should necessarily be expected to provide a complete ordering over states, rather than a partial means of classifying states.

Economists often extend the range of judgements which are possible using the Pareto criterion by reference to notions of hypothetical compensation.[15] If the gainers from some policy could, in principle, compensate the losers whilst retaining some net gain, the policy is declared a "potential Pareto improvement". Of course, if compensation is actually paid there is an actual Pareto improvement and the policy would be unanimously supported. The potential Pareto improvement is widely used as an indicator of an ethically desirable policy, but despite this common use the whole notion of hypothetical compensation is fundamentally opposed to the Paretian position, precisely because it attempts to trade off gains and losses between individuals.

The hypothetical compensation principle is consistent with an aggregative social welfare function approach which, as we have seen, can be viewed as a form of weighted utilitarianism. But any such principle must be viewed as anti-Paretian in that it violates the basic view on the strong incommensurability between individuals.

Paretianism is often portrayed as a minimalist ethic in the sense that it is claimed to be difficult to imagine an ethical theory which would not agree with Paretian judgements in circumstances where the ,Pareto criterion is decisive. However, this portrayal is misleading. Paretianism does accept welfarism and consequentialism and, as we have seen, both of these views are contentious. It is therefore clearly possible to imagine ethical views which might contradict Paretian judgements and so challenge the claim that Paretianism involves only minimalist value judgements. More detailed discussion of conflicts between Paretianism and other commonly accepted ethical views will be discussed in later sections.

The principal attraction of Paretianism to economists is the correspondence between the equilibria of idealised market economies inhabited by perfectly rational individuals and positions of Pareto optimality. This correspondence is sometimes taken as a striking proof of the social desirability of a market system, or of the social efficacy of individually self-interested behaviour; but in fact this correspondence is better seen as an example of the possible harmony of definitions. Perfect rationality, as we have seen, ensures that each individual achieves the maximisation of his own interests, which are elevated to ethical status by welfarism and protected by the Paretian power of veto. Meanwhile, the idealised market situation is precisely that which rules out consideration of any situations of the prisoners' dilemma type in which strategic considerations might constrain individual rationality's ability to maximise utility.

The result of a correspondence between the equilibria of such economies and Pareto optimality is powerful not because it demonstrates the ethical superiority of markets, or the ethical value of self-interest, but precisely because it clearly demonstrates the intimate linkages which exist between concepts of rationality and ethics. The result indicates the nature of the restrictions which have to be placed on the operation of the social economy in order to bring two carefully chosen definitions which reinforce each other directly into perfect alignment.

Another view which shares the Paretian emphasis on the role of unanimity, but is otherwise distinct, may be termed Wicksellian or procedural individualism.[16] This view rejects both welfarism and consequentialism as well as sum-ranking, and so makes a clean break with utilitarianism. The Wicksellian individualist argues that abstract or idealistic notions of the good — whether at the individual or the social level — are essentially arbitrary. Individuals, in this view, are seen not only as the best judges of their own interests but also, and more fundamentally, the only sources of ethical values. So the unanimity criterion is supported as a guarantee of respect for each individual's own ethical views.

This view can, I believe, best be understood in the context of the meta-preference ranking view of extended rationality discussed in the preceding chapter. Whilst the Paretian — via welfarism — takes the individual's common utility function as ethically relevant, the Wicksellian takes the individual's meta-preference as the only appropriate basis for ethical judgement. The Wicksellian view is then one of ethical relativism that allows individuals distinct ethical views which are to be equally respected. Given this, it is clear that the Wicksellian view is procedural rather than substantive in nature, and that no single, particular substantive view of ethics can emerge from Wicksellian individualism.

3.4 LIBERALISM

Wicksellian individualism can be viewed as a form of liberalism,[17] and many other variants of liberalism have been actively discussed in the political economy literature in recent years.[18] I shall not attempt to survey this literature.[19] Instead, I shall concentrate initially on the notion of individual freedom which is a central concept in all variants of liberalism, and view the various "liberal" approaches to freedom. A second theme will be the nature of the arguments used to support liberal views of freedom. Finally, I shall discuss the possible tension between liberalism and Paretianism which arises out of their separate views on individualism.

The basic distinction between positive and negative

freedom is by now a traditional starting point for the discussion of liberal attitudes to freedom.[20] Negative freedom arises from the absence of any coercion originating in the action of other individuals or groups of individuals, whereas positive freedom is a measure of ability to do things and may be diminished by all manner of constraints independent of human action. The classic liberal approach to freedom concentrates on negative freedom and argues that it is an important — even paramount — social principle. Thus, for example,

Liberalism as we understand the concept is concerned essentially, though not exclusively, with the maintenance of individual freedom, defined as the condition of mankind in which coercion of some individuals by others is reduced to the minimum possible degree. (Rowley and Peacock, 1975, p. 78)

The next stage in the classic liberal argument is the recognition that coercion cannot be totally eliminated. The Hobbesian "state of nature" characterised as a war of each against all is seen as a coercive environment, and in escaping from this position society must use coercive powers to limit the extent of coercion. In Hayek's words:

Coercion, however, cannot be altogether avoided because the only way to prevent it is by the threat of coercion. Free society has met this problem by conferring the monopoly of coercion on the state and by attempting to limit this power of the state to instances where it is required to prevent coercion by private persons. (Hayek, 1960, p. 21)

Most, if not all, liberals would go along with the argument to this point. However, a number of possible routes are available to continue the argument. The next step of the argument must provide a reason for valuing (negative) freedom. Two broad positions are possible here: freedom might be seen as an end in its own right or as a means to some further end.

If freedom is valued as an end, all that remains is to argue about the existence of other, co-ordinate ends and the possibility of trade-offs between these various ends. This line of argument is taken by Rowley and Peacock who write that: "freedom is not a means to a higher political end, but itself the highest political end" (Rowley and Peacock, 1975, p. 80).

This denies the possibility of trading freedom off against other, lesser political ends, although Rowley and Peacock do identify a hierarchy of freedoms and explicitly allow for trade-offs within this hierarchy.[21] Rawls' position of ranking maximal equal liberty lexicographically prior to any further end provides the best-known example of treating freedom as an end and specifying its logical relationship with other ends.

If, on the other hand, freedom is seen as a means to some other end, it becomes necessary to specify this end, and to discuss the possibility of other means to it. In one passage Hayek seems to advance this line of argument,[22]

Our faith in freedom does not rest on the foreseeable results in a particular circumstance but on that belief that it will, on balance, release more forces for the good than for the bad. (Hayek, 1960, p. 32)

This passage indicates that freedom may produce both good and bad "forces" — and so freedom cannot be an end in itself. Furthermore, the fact that the good dominates the bad "on balance" is put as the reason for "our faith in freedom", indicating an instrumental and essentially consequentialist view of freedom. Unfortunately, there is little in Hayek's surrounding discussion to suggest what the good brought about by freedom might be — it is certainly not a concept of utilitarianism, which is heavily criticised by Hayek as "constructivist". Yet, without a more detailed specification of the good, and the causal link between freedom and the good, this version of the liberal argument is severely weakened.

One possible version of the good associated with Mill,[23] and present to some extent in Hayek, is the argument that freedom is required to allow "experiments in living" and to allow individuals to develop their full potential. This argument is put by Mill in the essay *On Liberty*, but elsewhere in the same essay freedom is defined as a means to the utilitarian end — albeit the non-welfaristic utilitarianism which allows Mill to "regard utility as the ultimate appeal on all ethical questions; but it must be utility in the largest sense, grounded on the permanent interests of a man as a progressive being" (Mill, 1910, p. 74). So the question remains whether a non-utilitarian argument for the "experiment in living" version of liberalism can be established.

These brief views of the alternative conceptions of freedom as end and as means are illustrative of a deeper division in the argument for liberalism.[24] On one side of this divide — that which sees freedom as a means — the argument is essentially teleological in that some supposition about individual ends and their ethical significance must be made. However, arguments of this form can only provide a second-order and conditional claim for freedom rather than the unconditional claim normally associated with liberalism, so teleological theories cannot be fully liberal in the libertarian sense.

The full liberal argument must be one which places freedom as an end in itself and which eschews teleological arguments in favour of a deontological position in which freedom arises as a right or set of rights defined independently of, and logically prior to, any conception of the good. This conception of deontological, rights-based liberalism can be seen to flow from the Kantian tradition.

Having established that full or unconditional liberalism must take this deontological form, it still remains to identify an argument generating and supporting such a view. A number of arguments of this type have been put in recent years, each with its own detailed view of precisely which rights are fundamental and which freedoms are thereby protected, and — more fundamental still — precisely what ensures the origin of these rights.

The major works by Rawls (1971), Nozick (1974) and Buchanan (1975b) each present an attempt at providing a deontological basis for liberalism.[25] Each therefore needs as a starting point a method of establishing rights which is independent of any conception of the good. In short, each needs an Archimedean point from which ethical judgements can be made. The notion of an Archimedean point parallels the idealised observer argument for utilitarianism outlined above (Section 3.2); however, the criticisms which point out that the idealised observer takes into account the individual's ends and "conflates all persons into one" clearly rules this particular construction out of consideration as a suitable Archimedean point for the deontological project.

Rawls' (1971) suggestion in this context is the creation of a hypothetical "original position" which defines a circumstance removed from any empirical consideration of individuals' ends or other characteristics. This original position forms the setting for an agreement amongst hypothetical individuals which acts to create the structure of rights which will then condition real society. Liberalism, according to Rawls' argument, is then the major outcome of a social contract. We will view the contractarian basis of Rawls' argument in the next section — we merely note for the present that the essential role of the contract made in the original position is the provision of an Archimedean point.

Nozick (1974) offers two distinct lines of argument in support of his particular version of the liberal, minimal state. The first and major line of argument, put in Part One of the book, is based squarely on the Lockean conception of the state of nature in which natural rights are well defined and fully recognised, although they may frequently be breached in the absence of enforcement. This state of nature, and the natural rights which are defined therein, provides the grounding for all subsequent ethical judgement.

In outline, Nozick's argument claims that a minimal, night-watchman state will emerge from the invisible hand process of private attempts to enforce pre-existing rights. Private protective agencies will be established and the nature of the good "enforcement" will lead to the existence of a single dominant protective agency. This agency becomes a state because of its *de facto* monopoly position and its moral obligation to compensate non-members (Nozick, 1974, pp. 108–18). Note that the payment of compensation is essentially similar to buying the agreement of non-members to the legitimacy of the state (as in the Paretian notion of actual compensation). If actual agreement is not required, the agency/state faces the daunting task of determining the appropriate level of compensation objectively.

This argument holds that enforcement has the character of a public good and justifies the state. However, other public goods may not be supplied publicly by recourse to a similar argument since, in Nozick's view, state provision of other public goods will inevitably involve redistribution and so violate some individual rights. Enforcement is seen as the only rights-protecting function of the state and all other possible functions are argued to be rights-infringing.

This line of argument places particular strain on two points. The first concerns the nature and origin of the rights being protected. Rights, in Nozick's view, are fully voluntarily transferable so that a situation is rightful if it derives from a earlier rightful situation by voluntary process. This clearly establishes Nozick's historical (as opposed to end-state) criterion of evaluation. But there is no substantial theory of rights acquisition in Nozick's work which goes beyond the Lockean state of nature. The origin of rights is discussed[26] but, in Nozick's terms, only the "general outline" of a theory of rights acquisition is offered and the crucial task of providing a "specific theory" is not attempted. In a sense this leaves us with a deontological argument which lacks an Archimedean point, but proceeds on the assumption that some method of justifying "natural" rights can be provided.

The second major load-bearing point in Nozick's first line of argument is the thoroughgoing incommensurability required to establish that the pre-existing rights of individuals should be seen as absolute constraints on society, rather than as items of value which may nevertheless be traded off against some conception of the social good. The argument for incommensurability used by Nozick again serves to underline the individualistic and deontological and approach.[27] Individualism implies that there is no social entity which can itself experience good. Thus, any infringement of an individual's rights in the name of the socal good must, in fact, be an infringement for the benefit of some other individual or individuals. If this is the case the individual whose rights are infringed is being used as a means to further the ends of another. Such a sacrifice of a right for the ends of another which, at best, contributes to the social good, is contrary to the basic deontological insistence on the priority of the right. Incommensurability, which protects rights from such potential sacrifices is, therefore, seen to follow naturally from the deontological approach.

The second and minor line of argument which Nozick offers, in Part Three of the book, moves somewhat closer to the Rawlsian theoretical position by adopting a variant of the contractarian perspective. In this argument, an Archimedean point is provided by an imaginative act of agreement which, Nozick argues, generates the same ethical views and implications as the first argument outlined above. Again, we will view the contractarian aspect of Nozick's work in the next section.

In parallel with Nozick, Buchanan (1975) provides two lines of argument. His major conception of the Archimedean point is once again a contractarian one which, in this case, is argued to support the Wicksellian individualist position outlined above. The contractarian setting in this case differs from Rawls' hypothetical original position and from Nozick's imaginative introspection by being based on a subjectivist view of uncertainty and a sharp distinction between the constitutional and post-constitutional levels of discourse. Once again the details of the contractarian argument will be studied in the next section.

The second line of argument associated with Buchanan is reminiscent of Nozick's non-contractarian defence of liberalism outlined above.[28] Buchanan offers a view of the process of society formation and the emergence of the state which begins in a Hobbesian state of nature. This argument takes the natural equilibrium of the anarchic situation as a starting point for the process of voluntary exchange of holdings (rights) which leads to both a protective and a productive state.[29] The parallel with Nozick is clear. Nozick's use of natural rights as the basis for a voluntary exchange theory of entitlement is open to the criticism that essential arbitrariness of the starting point removes any claim to justification which the procedural argument might otherwise have.[30] This same criticism can be levelled at Buchanan. The natural equilibrium of an anarchic war of each against all may be of considerable descriptive value in the study of anarchy, and may equally form the basis for a positive theory of the emergence of certain institutions (see Section 4.2). But unless this natural equilibrium can be justified as an Archimedean point it must be taken to be just as arbitrary as Nozick's natural rights position, and just as unsuitable as a starting point for the deontological project.

The different specifications of the relevant Archimedean points adopted by Rawls, Nozick and Buchanan produce distinct versions of liberalism. Rawls adopts an end-state criterion, whilst both Nozick and Buchanan emphasise the historical nature of their criteria. Rawls places liberty lexicographically above further and well-specified elements of social good.[31] In this way Rawls can be argued to preserve the incommensurability required by the deontological view. Meanwhile, as we have already seen, Nozick is firm in ranking liberty and the priority of right lexicographically over any unspecified view of the social good. Buchanan also places liberty as an incommensurable, but on the slightly different grounds that there can be no view of the further social good except that which is expressed by free individuals.

Whilst the visions of liberalism held out by these three authors are distinct from each other in many important details, they all share the basic deontological structure which I have emphasised as the hallmark of the fully liberal position. In this context it is interesting that the search for an Archimedean point from which rights can be justified has led each of these authors to contractarian positions, although here again, as we shall see, their detailed positions vary quite considerably.

Liberalism is often taken to be a doctrine which indicates the supremacy of a particular social order with a small and heavily constrained government acting as a night-watchman for an unconstrained market economy. This view is clearly put in the writings of Hayek (1960, 1973, 1976, 1979), Nozick (1974) and Rowley and Peacock (1975) amongst the authors discussed above; but both Rawls and Buchanan may be distanced from this view in at least some respects.

Rawls attempts to combine (lexicographically) a deontological defence of liberalism with a further specification of the social good which — as we shall see in the next section — is reminiscent of a particular version of weighted utilitarianism. By specifying this further conception of the social good Rawls certainly removes his brand of liberalism from the simple vision of the free market.[32] Similarly, Buchanan, by focussing entirely at the procedural level, allows for outcomes which may lie anywhere on the spectrum which ranges from the free-market to the government controlled, depending upon the meta-preferences of individuals in pre-contractual society.[33]

Having viewed the nature of some arguments which have been deployed in support of liberal positions, I now turn to the final theme of this section — the possible conflict between liberalism and Paretianism. The starting point for this discussion is the claim by Sen (1970) of the "impossibility of the Paretian liberal".[34] This claim is that individual preference rankings can be found such that the simultaneous requirements of Paretianism and a system of individual rights which is characterised as liberal or libertarian, imply that no consistent social choices can be made. The particular system of rights studied in Sen's theorem is such that at least two individuals are each given unconditional rights to make a decision between one pair of alternatives. Sen's conflict is illustrated in Table 3.4, which details the preferences of two individuals over four possible social states. Let the rights structure be that A has the unconditional right to choose between x and y, whilst B has the unconditional right to choose between w and z. In this situation, w is unanimously preferred to x, and y is unanimously preferred to z; at the same time y is rejected by A whilst w is rejected by B. Society if left with no choice. If it wishes to respect individuals' rights it must choose a state which is Pareto inferior, and any Pareto improvement must infringe someone's rights.

Nozick has responded to Sen's argument by stressing the deontological justification of rights which places them prior

Table 3.4: The Paretian Liberal

Individual	A	B
1st Preference	w	y
2nd Preference	x	z
3rd Preference	y	w
4th Preference	z	w

to any theory of the good such as Paretianism: "Rights do not determine a social ordering but instead set the constraints within which a social choice is to be made" (Nozick, 1974, p. 166).

Thus the deontological liberal's reaction to our example must be to restrict social choice to the set of alternatives (x, z). But the important word in the last sentence is "social". Social choices interpreted as collective decisions must, on the deontological view, respect individual rights; but the individuals who hold those rights may trade them away or abandon them at will. Thus the liberal need not argue that x or z should be the final outcome of all choices; raher he should argue that one of these states should be the outcome of social choice and the starting point for purely individual choice. In fact, in our example, individual action can be expected to move society from the starting point to a Pareto optimal position. For example, if x is socially chosen, B may be expected to abandon his right to reject w and so allow the Pareto improvement to w since he himself gains from his move. The point is that whilst B may do this, society may not.

Of course in some situations individual choices may not move society from the socially chosen, right-respecting starting point to a Pareto optimum. The prisoners' dilemma is one situation in which strategic considerations may prevent individuals from exercising their private rights over the choice of action in such a way as to ensure a Pareto optimal outcome. Here the liberal must argue that it is illegitimate for society — in the body of government — to coerce individuals to adopt the cooperative strategy on threat of punishment, whilst it would be perfectly legitimate to set up institutions which could enforce privately made contracts where individuals voluntarily precommit themselves to cooperation. The distinction then is not concerned with the desirability of cooperation, but with the legitimacy of means of achieving cooperation.

An alternative perspective on the debate between Paretianism and liberalism can be gained by viewing the powers of veto offered by each criterion. The Pareto criterion provides each individual with a veto over all choices, whilst liberalism grants immunity from the veto power of others over particular choices involving rights. Such immunities must conflict with the general right of veto unless they are taken as deontologically prior constraints. If this is allowed then such conflicts as may arise concern the allowable means to social outcomes, and the possibility of encountering prisoners' dilemma type situations in which individual rights prevent the direct enforcement of Pareto optimal solutions.

3.5 CONTRACTARIANISM

We have seen in the preceding section that essentially contractarian positions have been widely used to provide grounds for substantively liberal ethical views. However, there is nothing in the nature of contractarianism *per se* which generates specifically liberal ethics. The defining characteristic of the contractarian approach is the identifiction of ethical values with the outcomes of particular types of agreements between individuals. In this way the contractarian concentrates on the circumstances of agreement in order to draw out substantial ethical propositions by inference.

Contractarianism involves two major themes which will be taken up separately in this section. The first concerns the internal structure of contractarianism and its search for a detailed specification of the relevant Archimedean point. This theme is informed by the fundamental question of the source of authority within the contractarian process.

In Chapter 2 we saw that prior agreement did not necessarily impose obligation upon the individuals who were party to the agreement. The central question within the first theme of contractarianism concerns this problem and the possibility of establishing a contract-situation such that the agreement which flows from it — whatever it may be — carries ethical weight.

The second theme concerns the translation from contractarian process to ethical outcome — from the Archimedean point to a substantive ethic. Here the questions concern the possibility of identifying particular outcomes of the contract process.

Discussion of both of these themes will centre around the distinctions between the work of Rawls, Nozick and Buchanan and, equally importantly, their similarities. Rawls' version of the contractarian process is strictly hypothetical,[35] involving the construction of an imaginary group of individuals set in unreal circumstances. Rawls' task is to provide a justification of the specification of the original position as an Archimedean point, and then to derive ethical principles from that specification.

In outline, the Rawlsian original position is one in which individuals are stripped of all their particular interests, desires and special knowledge in order that they can be seen to be in a situation in which all are equally informed about the nature of society without being informed at all about their own particular position or roles within society.[36]

One excludes the knowledge of those contingencies which sets men at odds and allows them to be guided by their prejudices. In this manner the veil of ignorance is arrived at in a natural way. (Rawls, 1971, p. 19).

How then does this doubly hypothetical construction claim ethical authority as an Archimedean point? Rawls' answer to this question is that the original position and the hypothetical individuals who populate it are, by construction, such that real individuals will accept them as reasonable, in the sense that they ensure objectivity and recognise the autonomy of individuals. This provides the final link in an argument that comes full circle to ground the Archimedean point of the original position in a form of simple contract between real individuals. But before we can fully recognise this final link, we need to introduce the idea of a reflective equilibrium.

The notion of reflective equilibrium[37] is crucial to understanding Rawls' argument. It may be sketched as follows. An individual has a certain intuitive notion of ethical justice and also an image of a hypothetical original position from which an ethical principle may be derived by contractarian process. The intuition will inform the design of the hypothetical position and, equally, the principle deriving from the hypothetical position may cause the individual to revise his intuition. Only when this process of redesign and revision is stationary, so that the hypothesised original position is consistent with the intuititive ethical view, which in turn suggests the hypothesised position, is the individual in reflective equilibrium. Note that this view of reflective equilibrium as a type of mental state on the part of an individual is also a view of reflective equilibrium as a particular bargaining outcome. Since the individual imagines a hypothetical contractarian process as a part of the iterative procedure which defines a reflective equilibrium, we may think of a reflective equilibrium as the outcome or equilibrium of such an individualistic, hypothetical bargain.

Of course, such an equilibrium may not be unique, as Rawls clearly indicates: there may be many ethical theories, each of which embodies a reflective equilibrium.[38] But Rawls argues that theories with this property have a special claim to justification. If a specification of an original position can be found which both justifies and is justified by a particular ethical view, then this ethical view must pass Rawls' test as a contractual theory embodying a reflective equilibrium.

The reflective equilibrium notion serves to ground the original position in the ethical intuitions of real individuals, which are themselves generated from the original position. This fact provides Rawls with an answer to a criticism put by several authors.[39] This criticism amounts to the argument that even if we, as real individuals, accept that the hypothesised agreement would emerge from the original position, this places no obligation on us since, in fact, we did not agree to these principles. Rawls might respond by pointing again to the concept of reflective equilibrium which implies that we, as real individuals, do actually accept the original position as relevant precisely because it fits well with our own ethical intuitions. The contractarian device, in Rawls' interpretation, modifies intuitions until a reflective equilibrium is reached and thereafter it reinforces intuition, so that the Rawlsian hypothetical contract is argued to bind real individuals in the very direct sense that they do actually agree with its principles. Of course, this argument is a general one which provides justification for any reflective equilibrium. Only if real individuals approach the same reflective equilibrium will there be widespread agreement on the authority of the ethical view involved. It is in this sense that the Rawlsian notion of contractarianism is ultimately dependent upon a simple contract of agreement amongst real individuals — each in a state of reflective equilibrium.

Both Nozick and Buchanan adopt a variety of contractarianism distinct from Rawls', which may be termed prospective contractarianism. A major part of the distinction between prospective and hypothetical contractarianism is that the social contract in both Nozick and Buchanan is argued to take place directly amongst real individuals in choice-situations which are distinguished from day-to-day decision-making by an imaginative step.

In Nozick this imaginative step is quite literal, since each individual is conceived as dreaming a world of his own, subject to the constraint that others have the same powers of creative dreaming:

If they choose to leave your world and live in another, your world is without them. You may choose to abandon your imagined world, now without its emigrants. This process goes on; worlds are created, people leave them, create new worlds, and so on. (Nozick, 1974, p. 299)

The notion of a stable or equilibrium world is then a world in which no one could imagine a subjectively better, feasible world. This is Nozick's vision of Utopia, which arises out of a procedure of contractual bargaining but is not described as any particular social system.

For Nozick, the Archimedean point which justifies Utopia is the bargaining game between real individuals, each pursuing their own ends but constrained by the ends of others.

Buchanan's view of contractarianism is essentially similar to this aspect of Nozick's analysis.[40] Buchanan again places real individuals at the hub of the contractarian process but uses a distinction between the constitutional level of discourse and the post-constitutional, together with a subjectivist discussion of uncertainty, to replace Nozick's imaginative dreaming.

At the constitutional level, individuals are concerned to select the structure of society in the face of widespread uncertainty concerning the future. Since uncertainty is interpreted as the unknowable rather than the merely probabilistic, this perspective recreates some aspects of Rawls' original position by enforcing a natural veil of ignorance.[41]

In Buchanan's conception, individuals in this constitutional state may have a variety of ethical views. Indeed, we may return to the notion of Wicksellian individualism and our discussion of rationality to indicate that individuals may be conceived as having the hierarchy of commitments associated with the extended view of rationality, so that the eventual social contract derives as the equilibrium of a bargaining game between ethical individuals facing constitutional uncertainty.

Just as Rawls ultimately grounds his conception of the Archimedean point in real individuals and their ethical intuition, so Buchanan also places individual ethical views at the centre of his scheme of justification, though by a more direct route.

If we set aside Nozick's Lockean discussion and Buchanan's Hobbesian discussion as being attempts to build deontological theories without an Archimedean point (Section 3.4), we are left with the prospective contractarian views outlined above. In this area, Nozick establishes his Archimedean point in the self-interested individual accepting other individuals as constraints at the equilibrium of a bargaining game; whilst Buchanan places his Archimedean point in the ethically aware individual facing a constitutional bargain with others and searching for equilibrium behind a natural veil of ignorance.

This picture of three views of contractarianism is one of convergence on several important points. Each author utilises a notion of equilibrium in a bargaining situation in which each individual has a veto as a major element in the claim for justification. Each author stresses the procedural nature of the contractarian perspective with the actual outcome of the process taking on a secondary importance. Finally, each author seeks to build the choice of ethical criteria on to the model of individual choice and, hence, on to a notion of individual rationality.

Rawls is explicit in formulating his view around rational choice.

The merit of the contract terminology is that it conveys that idea that principles of justice may be conceived as principles that would be chosen by rational individuals. (Rawls, 1971, p. 16)

Nozick and Buchanan, in the nature of prospective contractarianism which places real individuals in the contractual process, must also stress this link between individual rationality and the formulation of ethical criteria.

Given this convergence, it is fair to conclude that each of these views of contractarianism seeks to locate its Archimedean point within the individual and, more specifically, within a notion of individual rationality.

We now turn to the second theme of the section — the derivation of particular principles from the contractarian process. Given our discussion so far, it is clear that if the three views of contractarianism are to come up with distinct principles — as they do — this must be due to the adoption of distinct views of individual rationality, and the differences in the circumstances of agreement between the three theories.

The appropriate starting point for this discussion is a general view of the nature of equilibria in bargaining situations. The central notion here is that of the "core" of a bargaining game. This idea may be sketched as follows.[42]

Imagine a situation in which a set of N individuals must divide a cake of fixed size among themselves. Each individual has a veto which provides him with some bargaining power. But what form does this veto take? It could be that each individual may withdraw from the bargaining process and take with him some specified slice of cake. Clearly then any bargaining solution must give each individual at least as much cake as is provided by the withdrawal option. Any bargain which satisfies these constraints and therefore rules out the possibility of any individual or coalition of individuals benefiting from withdrawal, is said to be in the core of the bargaining game. Thus the core consists of all allocations which cannot be blocked by the withdrawal of some coalition. In general, the core will contain many possible equilibria.

The essential point is that the definition of the core, and therefore of the equilibria of the bargaining game, depends crucially upon the specification of the withdrawal rule which determines the capabilities of individuals and coalitions of individuals to block particular outcomes. How does this description of the core relate to the discussion of bargaining equilibria in each of the contractarian views outlined? We may take each author in turn.

Reflective equilibrium was the central notion in the Rawlsian view together with the idea that in a fully specified original position the outcome should be fully determined by a consideration of rational choice. Translating this into the language of bargaining games, this implies a search for a withdrawal rule which supports an outcome which is, in the relevant sense, consistent with the original withdrawal rule. The withdrawal rule is here taking the role of ethical intuition whilst the formal bargaining game is identified with the hypothetical contract process in the original position. Reflective equilibrium then demands consistency between withdrawal rule and bargaining outcome in the sense that each must support the other.

The situation can be exemplified in the case of the cake-sharing bargain discussed above. If the withdrawal rule is that each individual can withdraw with 1/Nth of the cake, then this rule clearly reproduces itself as the only feasible bargaining outcome. But this is not a unique reflective equilibrium. Any withdrawal rule which gives withdrawal shares to the individuals such that they sum to unity will also be a reflective equilibrium, thereby illustrating the multiplicity of equilibria in even the simplest bargaining model.

Of course, in this simple example the withdrawal rule and the bargaining outcome are identical, rendering the notion of bargaining trivial. More generally the notion of reflective equilibrium simply requires consistency between intuition and bargaining outcome in the sense that each supports the other.

This discussion helps us to understand the derivation of the particular principles of justice in Rawls. Consider the difference principle, which is argued to flow from the original position as a principle of justice which operates once liberty has been assured. The difference principle effectively states that inequalities in the distribution of primary goods are to be allowed only to the extent that they favour the worst-off group in society.[43] What withdrawal rule would support and be supported by this bargaining outcome?

The first point to note is that, in contrast to our cake-sharing example, the size of the social product to be distributed across individuals is not fixed; rather it depends upon individual incentives which depend in turn on the allocation rule to be utilised. It is this incentive problem that causes Rawls to move away from the requirement of strict equality.

A Rawlsian specification of a formal bargaining game is explored by Howe and Roemer (1981) who view the veil of ignorance as the crucial element of the Rawlsian analysis. The interpret the veil of ignorance as a form of lottery (with unknown probabilities) where the contracting individuals are randomly assigned places in society which endow them with characteristics — such as potential earning power, etc — and with incentive properties. The withdrawal rule specified by Howe and Roemer is that a coalition of individuals can block an allocation if it can guarantee its members an improvement in their positions in terms of primary goods by means of returning behind the veil of ignorance, making a new agreement and taking another drawing from the same lottery.[44] Howe and Roemer then prove that the outcome of the bargaining game defined in this way is precisely the set of maximin distributions discussed by Rawls.[45]

If reflective equilibrium is taken as the central device of Rawlsian contractarianism — as I have suggested — Howe and Roemer's model can only be considered fully Rawlsian if their specification of the withdrawal rule is fully consistent with and supported by the outcome of the bargain. That this is indeed the case is easy to see by viewing the coalition which consists of the worst-off group. This coalition could always guarantee its members an improvement by re-entering the lottery if there existed allocations in which the worst-off group was better situated than the coalition currently is. This coalition would then withdraw from all allocations except that which maximises the supply of primary goods to the worst-off group. And this is exactly the difference principle. The difference principle is therefore not just the equilibrium of a well-specified bargaining game — which is Howe and Roemer's point — but it is that rarer phenomenon, a reflective equilibrium, and it is this property which gives it a special claim to justification.

Ethical intuition is the mainspring of reflective equilibrium since it provides the starting point for bargaining — the equivalent of a withdrawal rule — but once ethical intuition enters the hypothetical contract it is refined by the process of rational bargaining. It may be objected that this interpretation of Rawls in bargaining terms is unfair since Rawls is careful to distance his argument from that of "bargaining in the usual sense" (Rawls, 1971, pp. 139–40); but this distancing arises from the specification of the circumstances of bargaining which are clearly anything but "usual", rather than any objection to the logic of bargaining, which must be of central importance to any contractarian viewpoint.

We now turn to consider the specification of rationality in Rawls' construct. It is clear from the characterisation of the veil of ignorance as a form of lottery which determines personal characteristics, skills, talents, etc, that these attributes are seen as inessential parts of the individual: mere possessions rather than constitutive elements. Indeed Rawls views such characteristics as forming a pool of common assets.[46] Thus, in one interpretation the individuals who are rational in Rawls' analysis are these "purified" individuals, stripped of all attributes. If this interpretation is accepted then these purified individuals are conceived as rational in the strict neoclassical sense of pursuing self-interest, even though they do not know the attributes which will determine the particular content of their self-interest.

Nozick is strongly critical of this view of purified individual rationality, arguing that an individual's talents and other characteristics must necessarily be seen as constituent parts of the person if rational choice is to be considered.[47] Furthermore, Nozick points out that Rawls must breach the fundamental deontological liberal code that individuals must be viewed as ends and not means if he allows individuals' attributes to be used as means.

Sandel (1982) offers a different line of argument in support of Rawl's view of common assets and of the difference principle. In this argument, rather than purifying the individual so as to retain the neoclassical concept of rationality, the opposite tactic of enriching the individual and adopting a broader concept of rationality is employed.[48] More precisely, individuals are conceived as having, as one of their constituent attributes, a sense of community which, in reflective equilibrium, is activated as a willingness to view assets as a common pool on the basis of a rational will to pursue individually grounded, but nevertheless communal, ends.

This view clearly relates back to the extended view of rationality discussed in the preceding chapter, which was represented in terms of meta-preferences with individuals recognising commitment to community as a vital part of their individualistic ends.

This approach to rationality within an otherwise Rawlsian framework could be seen as a counterbalance to Rawls' criticism of utilitarianism. If "utilitarianism does not take seriously the difference between persons",[49] then the purified-individual basis for Rawls' theory seems guility of not taking seriously the communal nature of society. The adoption of the broader view of individual rationality seems to allow for this commitment to community whilst still preserving the notion of reflective equilibria as the central justifying device.

In summary then, Rawls' view of individual rationality is that the "purified" individual is fully neoclassically rational whilst having the particular content of his preferences stripped away. I shall argue later (Section 3.8) that Rawls' notion of primary goods stands in place of individual preferences and allows the purified individual to be modelled wholly in terms of neoclassical means-rationality or consistency.

This discussion of the Rawlsian case provides a good background for a brief discussion of the views of Nozick and Buchanan.

Nozick, as we have seen, employs real individuals as the bargaining agents in his conception of the social contract, and sets out his bargaining game in terms of the imagination of other worlds subjects to the constraint of others having the same powers of imagination. Our task is then to translate this description into a specification of a bargaining game in order to view its properties.

First, Nozick argues that, since attributes such as skill are an integral part of the individual, each individual must be granted his marginal product — his marginal contribution to the social product. But this in itself does not provide a withdrawal rule sufficient to pin down the bargaining outcome in any detail.

It is plausible to suggest that the social product will not be exactly exhausted by providing each individual with his marginal product. Imagine a society of N individuals where each person is paid his marginal product, which is calculated by comparing the total product of the society of N with the total product in a society of $N-1$ which was without the particular individual. There is, of course, no guarantee that these N payments will exhaust the total product.[50] But if there is a surplus, how is it to be allocated? If the withdrawal rule for the bargaining game is simply that each individual can withdraw taking with him his attributes and therefore his marginal product, then there is no determinate solution to the problem of allocating the social surplus. Many allocation rules lie in the core.

If, in addition to their marginal products of labour, individuals could withdraw with a particular property entitlement, defined so that the sum of all entitlements exactly exhausts the available property, then the bargaining game becomes the full capitalist economic model and it is well known that perfectly competitive market equilibria lie in the core of this game.

This free-market outcome can be seen to be a reflective equilibrium since the intuition embodied in the withdrawal rule — private ownership of property and the returns from both property and labour — is reflected directly in the perfect competitive market outcomes which form the core of the model, which in turn support the withdrawal rule. In this sense, the Nozickian model corresponds to the Rawlsian criterion of justification by providing a reflective equilibrium. However, this interpretation of the Nozickian view requires the initial property-rights distribution embodied in the withdrawal rule to be based on ethical intuition rather than on any discussion of natural rights deriving from an abstract state of nature.

The implicit assumption running through this discussion of the Nozickian contract is, of course, that of perfect neoclassical, self-interested rationality. Only if this assumption is maintained will the bargaining games specified have the outcomes described. In contrast to Rawls, Nozicks' bargain is very much the "usual" one in which fully informed and fully rational individuals interact on the basis of conflicting interests to produce an equilibrium based on self-interest.

As has already been indicated, Buchanan's view of the contractarian process can be seen as intermediate between Rawls and Nozick in at least some respects. Real individuals are the actors in Buchanan's model just as they are in Nozick's, but the subjectivist interpretation of uncertainty provides a veil of ignorance which parallels that in Rawls.

However, a distinctive feature of Buchanan's discussion of the constitutional level of discourse is his unwillingness to derive explicit principles of social organisation or ethics from his formulation of the contractarian process. Certainly Buchanan articulates a presumption in favour of competition and free markets of the type strongly recommended by Nozick, but this presumption is not a strong prediction that such a market system must necessarily arise as the equilibrium of the relevant constitutional bargaining game. This lack of direct support for private rather than public decision-making is explicitly stated by Buchanan: "People may decide to do things collectively. Or they may not. The analysis, as such, is neutral in respect to the proper private sector–public sector mix". (Buchanan, 1964, pp. 221–2).

This feature of Buchanan's position reflects his subjectivism and the fact that, for Buchanan, the bargaining games actually contain real bargaining which cannot be predicted solely on the basis of a consideration of rationality.[51] The subjectivist element of Buchanan's discussion implies that individuals involved at the constitutional level cannot fully perceive the way in which alternative institutional structures will actually work, and furthermore that they may genuinely disagree in terms of the belief-models which underpin their rationality.

This heterogeneity of beliefs within the constitutional contract implies that the outcome of the bargain cannot be predicted. Instead, Buchanan uses Rawls' notion of pure procedural justice[52] to argue that, whatever institutional arrangements may flow from the constitutional contract, they must be justified as a result of the processes which generate them out of the Archimedean point of inter-personal agreement. This is Nozick's historical principle of evaluation but applied at the constitutional level itself.

Buchanan readily allows that individuals may be motivated by ethical values in addition to self-interest, and this suggests the extended view of rationality. However, the subjectivist discussion and the unwillingness to use an appeal to rationality to identify a particular bargaining outcome suggest that the imperfect version of the extended view of rationality underpins Buchanan's version of contractarianism.

3.6 MARXIAN ETHICS

Much of the modern debate on the Marxian interpretation
of ethics can be divided into two themes, one of which
revolves around Marx's discussions of justice and freedom
and their relationship to the central notion of exploitation;
whilst the other approaches exploitation via the debate on
the labour theory of value and the institution of private
property.[53]

The interpretation of Marx offered by Wood (1972, 1979)
draws a sharp distinction between justice and freedom.
Justice is seen as a part of the superstructure of society which
is dependent upon the underlying mode of production. In
other words, justice is viewed as a relativistic concept with
each form of society — feudal, capitalist, socialist, etc —
having its own concept of justice which is internally valid
but of no more general significance.

For Marx, justice is the property a transaction possesses when it stands
in a certain functional relationship to the mode of production in which
it takes place. It is a separate question whether, when and from whose
point of view just transactions are something valuable. (Wood, 1979, p.
269)

Freedom, on the other hand, is taken to be a firmer base
for inter-societal comparisons. However, freedom, in Marx,
is to be understood as freedom from exploitation rather than
freedom from coercion.[54] Exploitation stands condemned as
a barrier to freedom rather than because it is unjust, since
transactions and social arrangements which are perfectly
just in the context of a particular mode of production may
nevertheless be exploitative.[55]

Brenkert (1979) offers a discussion of the characteristics
of Marxian freedom which emphasises both the similarities
and the differences between this usage and the liberal usage
of the term. As a point of similarity Brenkert notes that in
the Marxian view, ". . . freedom exists when, through the
rational control and direction of the conditions of the existence, one develops his capacities and talents so that he may
do as he pleases" (Brenkert, 1979, p. 124). Whilst this has all

the appearance of a liberal statement, the quote continues: "Private property, in contrast, divides one's life activities not voluntarily, but naturally" (Brenkert, 1979, p. 124). Thus, freedom and private property are held in conflict by the claim that private property is not rationally or "voluntarily" based but rather depends upon some arbitrary or "natural" fact which then constrains freedom.[56]

A further aspect of the Marxian notion of freedom which differentiates it from the liberal conception is the idea that full freedom is possible only within a community,

People are genuinely free . . . only in cooperative, harmonious relations with others in which rational and voluntary control is exercised over their life activities. (Brenkert, 1979, pp. 127–8)

This is held in contrast to the liberal view which sees freedom in the inviolability of the individual insulated from relations with others.

That freedom from exploitation is a principal evaluative device in Marxian thought is clear; however, this raises two issues. First, how does freedom fit into any wider evaluative or ethical structure, and second, precisely what is the source of exploitation and how might freedom be increased?

On the first of these issues, interpretations of Marx differ. Whilst most would agree that Marx was not a utilitarian, the priority of freedom over justice and any other aspects of the good may not amount to a full incommensurability. We have already seen that freedom is a property defined over alternative socio-economic systems, whilst justice and other aspects of the good are defined only within a particular system. At any moment in time, and within any particular system, the degree of freedom may be commensurable with other values, but no trade-off will be possible as long as the socio-economic system is retained. On the other hand, between systems justice becomes incommensurable since there is no system-free definition to form a basis for comparison, and so freedom becomes the primary value in the choice between systems.

On the second issues, it is now widely — though by no means universally — agreed that the Marxian notion of exploitation is not most appropriately grounded in the labour theory of value, but rather finds its origins in the institution of private property itself.[57] In this property relations view of exploitation it is precisely the inequality of access to the stock of alienable property (capital) which describes the nature of the capitalist mode of production, and simultaneously ensures exploitation regardless of the precise nature of the relationships between the property-less and the property-owners. Even if there is no labour market and so no wage-employment — exploitation will result. This can be illustrated with an example from Roemer (1982a).

Suppose that there are two methods of producing the single consumer good in an economy. One method involves only labour and requires sixteen hours' work per day to sustain one person. The other method requires capital and needs just eight hours' labour to sustain one person and reproduce the capital. Now imagine that there is only enough capital to operate the second method to sustain one-half of the total population. If this capital were equally distributed each person would work twelve hours — eight on the labour-intensive method and four on the capital-intensive — in order to sustain himself. This position of full equality clearly involves no exploitation.

Now imagine that the capital is owned by one-half of the population, and is equally divided amongst that half. Several possibilities arise. One is that the capital owners each work eight hours and the property-less each work sixteen hours with no trade of any kind taking place between the two groups. A second possibility is that each capitalist hires a property-less worker to work on his capital, offering one-half of one day's subsistence for eight hours' work, keeping the other half of the output for himself. All of the property-less could be employed in this way and this would be the market equilibrium wage. In addition, everyone works a further eight hours in the labour-intensive method. The result of this second scheme is that each property-owner works eight hours and each property-less worker works sixteen hours — exactly as before — but now there has been an active labour market, and it appears that workers did not receive the full value of their product.

In each of these schemes involving unequal access to capital, Roemer argues that exploitation is present to an identical degree. The absence of the labour market in the first case is no barrier to the existence of exploitation, nor is that fact that the property-less person always has the option of working in the labour-intensive process so that he can be said to be working for the capitalist voluntarily or without coercion. The hallmark of exploitation is that one group — the exploited — is working more than is socially necessary to the advantage of another group — the exploiters — who are working less than is socially necessary, regardless of any particular market interaction between the two groups.

Nozick, in his discussion of Marxian exploitation, agrees with the property-relation definition of exploitation but argues that the voluntary nature of employment in this example denies the existence of exploitation:

. . . it is this crucial fact of non-access to the means of production that underlies exploitation, it *follows* that in a society in which the workers are *not* forced to deal with the capitalist, exploitation of labours will be absent. (Nozick, 1974, p. 254 — emphasis in original)

Roemer denies this point by effectively arguing that it is not "the crucial fact of non-access to the means of production" which is the prerequisite of exploitation, but the *unequal* access to the means of production. Our earlier discussion of the Marxian distinction between justice and freedom would allow us to agree with Nozick that the situation in Roemer's example is just, whilst still agreeing with Roemer that it is exploitative.

In a series of works,[58] Roemer has developed a game-theoretic analysis of the property-relations view of exploitation which allows direct comparison with the bargaining game analysis of contractarian positions outlined in the previous section. Given the definition of capitalist exploitation based on the existence of unequal holdings of private property, it is easy to see that a bargaining game specified by a withdrawal rule which allows individuals or coalitions to withdraw with their *per capita* share of the total stock of alienable property, will have as its core the set of non-exploitative outcomes.

This game, and its outcome, is strikingly similar to the Nozickian specification of the contractarian process. Each individual has a property entitlement under the withdrawal rule, and this entitlement delimits the core. If the equilibrium of such a game is to be interpreted as a Rawlsian reflective equilibrium, the property entitlement under the withdrawal rule must derive from individuals' ethical intuitions. If this intuition suggests that equal shares are appropriate then Roemer's game converges on Nozick's in reflective equilibrium.

If the language of reflective equilibrium is dropped, the question separating Nozick's and Roemer's specifications is which of the two withdrawal rules has the greater ethical significance, ie which forms an Archimedean point? Nozick's appeal here is to natural rights and a just process of rights transfer, whilst the Marxian analyst would claim these justifications to be bogus on the grounds that they have credibility only within a capitalist system. The egalitarian or "rationalist" rule would then be selected simply because it ensures the relevant freedom from exploitation as its outcome.

The general similarity between Nozick's and Roemer's formulation of the bargaining game is suggestive of a deeper relationship between the liberal notion of freedom which is the focus of Nozick's analysis and the Marxian freedom from exploitation studied by Roemer. Since Roemer's analysis provides the more restrictive withdrawal rule (specifying a particular property entitlement rather than just some property entitlement), it seems that the freedom from exploitation may entail freedom from coercion and go beyond this to guarantee some further freedom — perhaps the freedom of community.

It is important to note that the non-exploitative bargaining game specified by Roemer does not necessarily — or even plausibly — imply an entirely egalitarian outcome. Capitalist exploitation arises out of unequal access to alienable property, but unequal access to inalienable property is sufficient to ensure inequality. Under Roemer's specification individuals would still have different talents and different incentive structures and these will imply that the egalitarian withdrawal rule will generally result in an unequal — but non-exploitative — outcome.

This point provides two links between Roemer's discussion of capitalist exploitation and Rawls'. First, if incentives are important, something which looks superficially like exploitation will not necessarily be exploitative in Roemer's terms. For example, if a group of unskilled workers are employed by a capitalist who pays them a competitive wage which is less than the whole product of their labour, there seems to be *prima facie* evidence of exploitation; and certainly a labour value theorist would diagnose exploitation. However, if these workers were to withdraw equipped with their own skills and their *per capita* share of capital, there can be no presumption that they would be better off. If they are not, they could not block the original allocation, and the apparently exploitative situation would lie in the non-exploitative core.

This type of apparent but unreal exploitation may certainly produce inequality but this inequality is allowed provided that it is beneficial to the apparently exploited group — a proposition redolent of Rawls' difference principle.

The second link involves the concept of the pool of common property. Here Rawls goes one step further than Roemer by viewing not only alienable property as falling within a common pool, but also inalienable personal characteristics. There is, however, a distinction to be drawn between Rawls' and Roemer's use of the common pool. Roemer views the equal *per capita* share of the common pool as the relevant withdrawal rule, whilst Rawls uses the device of a lottery from behind the veil of ignorance to allocate unequal shares of the common pool. This distinction implies that the Rawlsian core may include equilibria which are exploitative in Roemer's sense.[59] Roemer studies cases in which personal characteristics are pooled and a withdrawal rule is specified in terms of a *per capita* share in the extended pool under the heading "socialist exploitation".[60]

The difficulties of establishing a clear view of the structure of Marxian ethics are considerable. Nevertheless, it is clear that freedom from exploitation must, on any reading of Marx, be a major part of the overall ethical objective. Despite the major differences in the rhetoric of the various parties to the debate, the objective of Marxian freedom has been seen to be capable of expression in the same format as the objective of the upholding of liberal rights. This ability of the contractarian device to provide links between such apparently dissimilar views will provide one base for our further discussion.

3.7   RIGHTS AND COMMENSURABILITY

The distinction between welfarism, sum-ranking and consequentialism made in the context of utilitarianism provides the basis for a broader comparison of the alternative ethical views outlined above. Welfarism is a theory about what has ethical significance, sum-ranking a theory about how items of ethical significance can be compared and aggregated, and consequentialism a theory of how actions can be ethically evaluated. Any ethical position must provide a discussion in each of these three areas.

Our previous discussions allow us to identify the two principal alternatives to welfarism as being a broader conception of the individual good, and rights — usually interpreted as protecting negative freedoms, freedom from coercion, exploitation etc. The principal alternatives to sum-ranking are the aggregative social welfare function which maintains full commensurability whilst relaxing strict additivity, and incommensurability. Finally, the principal alternatives to consequentialism are deontology or a compromise position which views acts as means and ends simultaneously.

Identifying three possibilities in each of the three theoretical areas identifies twenty-seven possible combinations, each of which could provide a class of ethical theories. However, as we have already seen, a number of these combinations are internally inconsistent. For example, full deontology implies incommensurability, and this in itself renders six of the combinations infeasible. Rather than discuss each of the feasible combinations I intend, in this section, to focus attention on the interrelated topics of rights and commensurability in an attempt to provide a point of comparison across alternative ethical views and to stress the crucial role of commensurability in distinguishing between viewpoints.

Sen (1982) argues that the fully consequentialist view of rights as mere means to some further end, and the deontological view of rights as constraints, share a weakness in that both views deny "that realization and failure of rights should enter into the evaluation of states of affairs themselves and could be used for consequential analysis of action" (Sen 1982, pp. 5–6).

The utilitarian consequentialist denies that the observance of rights is, in itself, of any ethical value. The libertarian deontologist denies that the value of rights observance depends in any way upon a consideration of consequences. This weakness, where the two views pass travelling in opposite directions, gives rise to intuitively unsatisfactory results in applying either view. Sen provides an example in which the only method of preventing a violent assault on A by B is for D to violate C's right to privacy.[61] The strict deontologist who views rights as constraints must argue that D should not violate C's right, since to do so would be to use C as a means — albeit a means to the protection of someone else's rights. This view is put by Nozick,[62] who also argues that all genuine rights must be co-possible.[63] Yet Sen's example is precisely one in which circumstances contrive to bring rights which are normally co-possible into conflict.

Sen extends the example by viewing the alternative scenario in which A is about to fall victim to some natural accident which will injure him to the same extent as the assault, but which will not violate his rights since no human agency is involved. D is still in the position of being able to save A from injury if and only if he violates C's right to privacy. The difference between the two cases must be irrelevant to the strict deontologist libertarian. D may not violate C's right for any reason. For the consequentialist utilitarian, the shift from assault to accident makes it more likely that D should intervene since B (who presumably gained from the assault) is no longer relevant. A third possibility is available. Rowley and Peacock (1975), in their statement of deontological liberalism, explicitly allow trade-offs between rights whilst disallowing any trade-offs between a right and any other aspect of the good. It is therefore possible that they might allow D to save A from assault, but not from accident.

The strict deontologist (Nozick) argues that each identified right is incommensurable in value with other rights or any non-rights value. The weak deontologist (Rowley and Peacock) suggests that rights may be commensurable in value with other rights but incommensurable with non-rights. The strict consequentialist must insist that only one scale of values exists, rendering all values commensurable.

Sen's discussion of these cases focusses on the distinction between rights observance as means and as ends. Consequentialism is seen as a concentration on end-states which denies direct ethical status to processes such as rights observance. Sen's suggestion, which he terms a goal-rights system, is to value rights as both means and ends, so that whilst ethical evaluation will still be partly consequence-based it will not be consequentialist. This suggestion is an effective way of strengthening the status of rights within the framework provided by Sen. However, this framework requires full commensurabiliy. On this aspect of the deontologist/consequentialist debate no compromise is possible — either values are commensurable or they are not. The Rowley and Peacock position which restricts the range of commensurability is an intermediate position of sorts, but it cannot compromise on the basic incommensurability between rights and other values. In this sense, Sen's goal-rights system is precisely a variant of the "utilitarianism of rights" which Nozick strongly criticises.[64]

If commensurability is allowed — as in Sen's approach — the criticism of not taking seriously the distinction between persons, originally aimed at utilitarianism, is reinstated. If rights merely contribute to some aggregate via an appropriate social welfare function, and the ethical imperative is expressed in terms of maximising this aggregate, then any individual's rights may be sacrificed to this ethical criterion.

If, on the other hand, commensurability is denied, any individual right acts as a veto on all other considerations and we must reconcile ourselves to situations, such as Sen's example, which may not reflect ethical intuition.

One apparent line of escape from this dilemma is to look again at the definition of rights in an attempt to argue that genuine rights do not produce cases which conflict with our intuitions. However, this line of argument holds no promise. For example, the freedom from arbitrary imprisonment is held as a genuine right by even the most restrictive negative rights theorist, and our intuition may generally support this right. But if we are told that imprisoning an innocent man for one hour is the only available method of certainly saving ten lives, then I, at least, would doubt the status of the individual's right to freedom as the only, incommensurable argument.

The ethical inflation which underlies this example simply points out that there can be (at most) only one ultimate value; any attempt to grant absolute priority to more than one right will automatically raise the possibility of counter-intuitive examples. This point brings into doubt the ethical significance of the distinction between positive and negative rights, and I shall return briefly to that topic below.

The dilemma which exists between commensurability, which in the final analysis submerges individuality, and incommensurability, which protects individuality at the expense of intuition, is a genuine one. There is no way of evading the issue and no way in which a compromise can be constructed. Of course, the incommensurability under discussion is not indicative of a simple inability to choose, since alongside the incommensurability we have a claim of absolute priority. It is the absence of any possibility of trade-off at the margin which is the hallmark of incommensurability.

How then could incommensurability arise? We may distinguish between intra-personal incommensurability and its inter-personal counterpart. At the intra-personal level we must refer back to the notion of rationality. Under the neoclassical view of rationality all values are subjectively commensurable, personal utility being the only criterion and motivator. If this view of rationality is correct then any social incommensurability must arise from the situation of intra-personal commensurability. In this view, it is not values which are incommensurable, but different people's values.[65] This case leads naturally to Paretianism, where the pattern of incommensurability follows the distinction between persons. By contrast, in the libertarian view the pattern of incommensurability follows the distinction between rights and mere interests within each individual, and this requires some further explanation.

If a neoclassically rational individual has a right, he does not view it as incommensurable with his interests. Indeed he is perfectly at liberty to trade off his own rights against his own interests — perhaps even to the point of selling himself into slavery.[66] If the individual does not recognise any incommensurability between rights and interests, how does it arise socially? Nozick points out that there are "some things individuals may choose for themselves, no-one may choose for another" (Nozick, 1974, p. 331). But why only *some* things? The point here is that if Nozick's claim is extended to *all* things, we are left with a strict Paretianism in which each individual is granted the right to a global veto. If only some things are protected by rights we have the additional difficulty of drawing the line of incommensurability. Two major possibilities arise. The first is to pursue the distinction between negative and positive rights referred to at the outset of the discussion of liberalism, in the hope that this will locate the boundary. The second is to pursue the idea of the social contract as an Archimedean point which justifies a particular allocation of rights. I shall return to these two possibilities shortly.

An alternative approach to inter-personal incommensurability is to return to the intra-personal level and dispense with the neoclassical view of rationality in favour of an alternative which embodies intra-personal incommensurabiliy in the form of lexicographic preferences. Once intra-personal incommensurability is established (if not argued for), the inter-personal equivalent may appear to be

easier to understand. This appearance is, however, decep-
tive. Unless all individuals share the same pattern of incommensurability, it is difficult to see how intra-personal incommensurability can translate into inter-personal or social
incommensurability except via the mechanisms put forward
in the case of neoclassical rationality. An abstract negative-
rights theory or a social contract seem to be the major
alternatives in either case.

These two potential sources of incommensurability are
fundamentally different. The negative-rights argument
operates by grounding incommensurability in absolute negative rights which are distinguished from positive rights on
the basis of their universalisability. Thus, it is claimed that
genuine (negative) rights relate to the basic notion of
rational human agency and so attach equally to all individuals. The social contract argument, on the other hand,
suggests that incommensurability will arise only to the extent
that it flows from an appropriately specified Archimedean
point in the form of absolute rights granted to individuals
in view of their membership of society. If no absolute rights
of membership are granted, then there is no incommensurability.

The difficulties in maintaining a sharp division between
positive and negative rights are considerable.[67] Some positive rights (eg to the means to subsistence) may be universalisable in a manner directly comparable to that of negative rights; and the notion that negative rights are costless
and co-possible in contrast with costly and conflicting positive rights is refuted once the costs of enforcement are taken
into account and situations of conflict such as Sen's example
recognised. Enforcement is probably the area in which the
negative-rights theory has its weakest link. If negative rights
are indeed incommensurably prior to welfare then the optimal amount of rights enforcement is that which reduces
rights infringement to zero, whatever the welfare cost. Thus
in the strictly libertarian society the night-watchman government would be empowered to expend whatever resources
are necessary to reduce all forms of rights enfringement to
zero. This may be a very considerable night-watchman.

On the other hand, if rights are not absolute and incommensurable a society may choose to balance the costs of enforcement against the costs of rights infringement at the margin, thereby identifying a socially "optimal" level of rights infringement which is non-zero.

I have argued above (Section 3.4) that deontological liberalism requires an Archimedean point. It follows from this that the contractarian approach to the justification of rights and incommensurability may be more appropriate than any attempt to overcome the difficulties of constructing an abstract negative-rights theory. However, the social contract is in no way constrained to grant absolute rights; conditional rights might emerge which preserve commensurability whilst defining the reservation price of the right in such a way as to afford the individual considerable protection in "normal" circumstances. This possibility moves towards Feinberg's view that, "To have a right is to have claim against someone whose recognition as valid is called for by some set of governing rules or moral principles. To have a claim, in turn, is to have a case meriting consideration" (Feinberg, 1970, p. 257). In this view a right is no more than a particularly strong, but clearly commensurable, argument.

The contractarian perspective provides the possibility of justifying incommensurability without guaranteeing it. We have already seen that the contractarian technique can provide a basis for a wide variety of ethical positions which differ from each other in various dimensions — commensurability is the starkest of these dimensions.

The dilemma of commensurability lies at the heart of much of the current ethical debate — as one might expect of an issue incapable of a compromise solution. We have seen how this debate relates to utilitarianism, Paretianism and liberalism, but the Marxian view of ethics centred on the notion of exploitation also depends upon a particular version of incommensurability, although in this case the incommensurability arises not between individuals, or between rights and interests, but between alternative economic systems or modes of production. This further emphasises the point that incommensurability may arise as a result of social organisation even though it is not present in any individual's evaluation of alternative states, since the latter are inevitably grounded within one particular social system.

A major advantage of the contractarian approach to rights is that it requires an explicit treatment of the linkage between the individually rational basis for contractarian agreement and the content of that agreement, which must itself take account of rational reactions to the institutions, laws and rights created. In this context rights can be seen as the result of individuals coming together to bind themselves to commitments which — to be credible — must spring directly from rationality. Thus, in a fully developed form, a contractarian argument simultaneously provides a justification of rights, a specification of their precise moral status, and an analysis of individualistic obligations to respect these rights. Unless individuals can be seen to be rationally committed to the substance of the contractarian agreement, there can be no duty or obligation incumbent on them, and the rights agreed in the contract process will have no special status in society.

Although I have not here developed anything like a full contractarian view of rights, I hope that I have done enough to suggest that the contractarian method — seen as a procedural technique — offers the most promising approach to the analysis of rights by leaving the question of commensurability open and allowing it to be settled by direct confrontation with a particular theory of rationality. The neoclassical theory of rationality seems to be a poor contender for this role in contractarian argument since it denies the relevance of obligation beyond self-interest. The imperfect and extended views of rationality will be argued to offer much better prospects.

3.8 RATIONALITY AND ETHICS

Just as negative rights theorists attempt to ground rights in the universalisable concept of rational human agency, so ethical theorists seek to provide the foundations for ethical criteria in rationality. Each of the approaches to ethics outlined in this chapter strives to establish the claim that the particular ethical criterion advanced corresponds to, or derives from, individual rationality.

The attempt to link rationality to ethics may take either of two general forms. In the first, individual rationality is regarded as basic and the role of ethics is to provide a framework which accommodates and protects rational behaviour. Any contrast between individual rationality and ethical desirability can arise only as a result of particular circumstances setting individuals in conflict with each other in strategic environments, and not as a result of any general tension between the two. The clearest example of this approach is Paretianism where, as we saw in Section 3.3, there is a harmony of definition between the neoclassical view of rationality and the Pareto criterion which can be disrupted only by the establishment of inter-personal dilemmas — such as the prisoners' dilemma — which drive a wedge between the operation of these harmonious definitions.

The second general approach to linking rationality and ethics is the use of a particular concept of rationality to derive an ethical position which, once derived, has independent status. Derivation may be either by deduction or by a consideration of individually rational choice. The separability argument for utilitarianism may be seen as an attempt to use the full neoclassical theory of rationality as a starting point from which to deduce an ethical position. Similarly the idealised observer argument for utilitarianism can be seen as an attempt to derive an ethical view from a consideration of individual choice.

The contractarian approach carries this last technique to its most general level. General contractarianism provides an analytic method which allows for the study of any particular view of individual rationality and its implications for collective ethics. Of course, it is not possible to move directly from a specific view of rationality to an ethical position; one also requires a discussion of the circumstances of choice which form the Archimedean point and some argument as to why this particular specification carries weight. But nevertheless, the principal momentum underlying contractarianism is the momentum from rationality to ethics.

In the Rawlsian version of contractarianism, the view of rationality utilised as the starting point amounts to little more than neoclassical means-rationality, with all particular forms of ends-rationality and belief-rationality transformed and homogenised by the veil of ignorance.[68] As we have seen (Section 3.5) individuals in the original position are conceived as being disassociated from their particular ends and beliefs, and yet are expected to make rational choices. This in itself serves to focus attention on means-rationality, and it is in this context that the notion of primary goods becomes important.

Primary goods are defined as those "things that every rational man is presumed to want" (Rawls, 1971, p. 62); so that primary goods are held to be of value to all individuals regardless of their (unknown) particular ends. In this way rational choice in the original position is concerned only with primary goods which stand in place of any particular substantive theory of ends-rationality.

Seen in slightly different terms, the Rawlsian appeal is that all substantive views of ends-rationality must agree on the value of certain goods, and that these (primary) goods take on a special significance. Rawls then replaces all particular views of ends-rationality with this lowest-common-denominator view which, by assumption, applies equally to all individuals. Given this treatment of ends-rationality, the focus of rational choice in the original position shifts back to means-rationality and the efficient pursuit of the common end.

Nozick's use of rationality in his contractarian argument is markedly different. Here the full neoclassical view of perfect rationality is employed in allowing each individual to design a Utopia constrained only by the freedom of exit of others. The ethical stance argued to follow from this use of full neoclassical rationality is a variety of liberalism which, at its limit, approaches Paretianism. The language of rights is unfamiliar to the Paretian, who uses the parallel language of voluntary agreement in its place; and the arguments used to support Paretianism and Nozick's liberalism are very different, as indicated by the discussion of teleological and deontological individualism in Section 3.4. But nevertheless, the two arguments converge in the limiting case where all of an individual's interests are protected as rights.

The distinction between Rawls and Nozick emphasised here is that Nozick employs a much more substantial concept of rationality than Rawls, corresponding to this use of a more substantial concept of the individual.[69] This difference explains much of the contrast between the two authors even though both work well within the neoclassical view of rationality.

Roemer's analysis of Marxian exploitation in a contractarian setting also utilises an essentially neoclassical view of rationality. Exploitation is excluded from the core of the bargaining game not by any appeal to non-individualistic motives held by the contracting agents, but rather by an appeal to the individual agent's rational self-interests in blocking allocations which made him worse off relative to the Archimedean benchmark. We have already noted the close similarity between the contract specified by Nozick and that of Roemer, which can be seen as exemplifying the multiplicity of equilibria normally available in bargaining games of this general type.

Each of the ethical theories reviewed so far in this section has been argued to utilise an essentially neoclassical view of rationality as its mainspring. The argument of Chapter 2 demonstrated that this view of rationality is subject to a broad range of criticisms, most of which are relevant to the use made of rationality in the derivation of ethical views. The imperfect rationality school of thought associated with Simon, Schelling and Elster which focusses on the self-recognition of irrationality and the adoption of rationality-improving second-best strategies, and the extended rationality line of argument developed by Sen and others in terms of a range of commitments going beyond self-interest, both carry strong implications for ethical theory. Nowhere are these implications stronger than in the contractarian tradition.

The status of neoclassical means-rationality interpreted as consistency is questioned by both imperfect and extended rationality. This would seem to provide a basis of criticism of the Rawlsian approach, but given the doubly hypothetical nature of the Rawlsian contract it is not clear that this further abstraction is damaging. On the imperfect rationality argument one might continue to support the assumption of perfect means-rationality in the Rawlsian original position, since the imperfect, real individual striving for rationality could be expected to hold perfect rationality as part of his ethical intuition and, therefore, as a part of the specification of the Archimedean point. Equally, on the extended rationality argument, the impact of extending rationality beyond self-interest would be felt in terms of the specification of primary goods, and since these are already viewed as valuable under *all* views of ends-rationality this cannot raise any additional difficulty.

It therefore seems as though the Rawlsian view, by avoiding any strong commitment to a particular view of rationality, also avoids a line of criticism. The Rawlsian equilibrium may continue to be an equilibrium under alternative views of rationality, but of course it will not be a unique equilibrium.

Nozick's and Roemer's analyses are much more open to modification in the light of reformulated views on rationality. If the specification of the bargaining game in terms of the withdrawal rule is retained, but an alternative concept of rationality is introduced, the core of the game can be expected to shift, as was suggested by the transformation of a prisoners' dilemma into an assurance game by the introduction of genuine altruism in Section 2.5. Of course a definite conclusion concerning the properties of the new core could only be reached by specifying the new form of rationality with some precision — but the point here is the simple one that Nozick's and Roemer's conclusions regarding the outcomes of their contractarian games are sensitive to changes in the specification of rationality.

Buchanan's contractarian position seems to be built on a view of rationality which lies outside the strict neoclassical tradition. Buchanan's subjectivism, and his continual emphasis on the process of contractarianism rather than its outcome, both suggest a position capable of embodying both the imperfect notion of rationality and the extended notion.

In this way Buchanan's subjectivist contractarianism, which places real, imperfect individuals at the heart of the contract process without specifying or limiting their rationality, can be seen as a general version of prospective contractarianism. Indeed, the obvious differences between Rawls and Buchanan in terms of their descriptions of the contract process are illustrative of the distinction between hypothetical and prospective contractarianism, but are otherwise largely superficial. The fact that neither specifies a particular narrow view of ends-rationality underlines the basic similarity of the two positions as far as the contractarian procedure is concerned.[70]

A general contractarian method, capable of operating either without a particular view of ends-rationality (Rawls) or with any appropriate view of the ends-rationality (Buchanan), provides a powerful device for generating alternative ethical views. However, this raises the obvious further question of the selection amongst these views. Clearly, since the views are themselves high-level evaluative criteria, it is implausible to search for further evaluative criteria by which to compare them. The only techniques available are those involving intuition and the examination of the process of derivation.

The role of intuition in ethics is much debated.[71] The full intuitionist may argue that it is impossible to analyse ethics in any meaningful way and that the only evaluative statements that can be made are those based directly on intuition, which may be mutually contradictory as between cases. In other words such an intuitionist denies the existence of rational ethics or of any link between rationality and ethics. Clearly, then, we cannot appeal to such intuitionism to evaluate what it rejects. The form of intuition which may be of some value in reinforcing analytic ethics is the form which accepts that in many areas intuition is uncertain, but accepts equally that a method of extending intuition into those areas by analytic means is of value. It is this form of intuition which is built into the notion of reflective equilibrium. To the extent that we have a strong and robust intuition on an ethical question, the analysis should confirm our intuition, but if the analysis points out inconsistencies in our intuition, then we may wish to reconsider our intuitions rather than insist immediately that the analysis is unhelpful.

The notion of reflective equilibrium — a balance between analysis and intuition — is an appealing device for screening the outcomes of bargaining games. But as we have already seen, the number of reflective equilibria may be large. If the same bargaining situation can produce a large number of reflective equilibria using alternative concepts of rationality, the only further screening device available is a judgement on the status of the alternative theories of rationality. This then is the examination of the process of derivation.

If the preferred view of rationality is still capable of multiple reflective equilibria — each representing an ethical system — then there is no further means of choice amongst them. This does not mean that the fact of multiplicity cannot be accounted for; indeed I shall argue in the next chapter that this fact is of considerable importance in considering the design of the institutions of state.

3.9 INTERIM CONCLUSIONS

The four alternative, substantive views of ethics outlined and reviewed in this chapter are all closely associated with economic doctrine. We have seen that the differences between the views can be characterised as lying in a number dimensions, of which we have focussed particular attention on three. These three dimensions can be summarised in terms of the polar contrasts between deontology and teleology, commensurability and incommensurability, and welfarism and rights. In terms of these three dimensions, the four ethical views can be crudely identified in Table 3.5. Whilst it is possible to achieve compromises along the deontological/teleological dimension and the welfarist/rights

Table 3.5: Substantive Ethical Views

Utilitarianism	— Teleological	— Commensurable	— Welfarist
Paretianism	— Teleological	— Incommensurable	— Welfarist
Liberalism	— Deontological	— Incommensurable	— Rights
Marxian	— Deontological	— Incommensurable	— Rights

dimension which permit a finer classification of positions, it has been argued to be impossible to identify meaningful compromises in the debate on commensurability. This leads to the identification of the dilemma of commensurability in which only the two "extreme" positions are logically available and yet each of these positions is intuitively unattractive. I have suggested that this dilemma is at the heart of much of the ethical debate.

A second theme of this chapter has been the role of rationality in the alternative views of ethics under discussion. We began this book by identifying the possibility of tension between individual rationality and a collective ethic. The naive presumption would be that these two forces were broadly independent of each other. Our discussion has now led us to the point where the links between individual rationality and alternative ethics are clearly observable. Although there is no simple one-to-one correspondence between views on rationality and views on ethics, a theory of rationality is a necessary input to a theory of ethics, and is often the input which acts to justify the claim to ethical significance. Rationality is a key feature of the Archimedean point.

Contractarianism then forms the third important theme of this chapter. I have argued that contractarianism — in its widest sense — provides a consistent framework for the investigation of alternative ethical claims and their dependence upon particular views of rationality. This view of contractarianism as a method follows in the tradition of Rawls and Buchanan whilst avoiding the particular substantive conclusion derived by Rawls, Nozick, or any other contractarian writer. In this sense, contractarianism is a device for generating and investigating ethical theories rather than a device for reducing the number of theories to one. As we have seen, the contractarian process is capable of producing a wide range of substantive ethical views, but this is its strength rather than its weakness. It is precisely the neutrality of the contractarian process as between substantive views which recommends it for use as an Archimedean point.

However, contractarianism is not a mere technique which draws its justificatory or ethical force only from the intuitive specification of the relevant bargaining situation. Contractarianism does carry within itself an element of justificatory force. The emphasis on agreement as a justifying procedure clearly presupposes a respect for individuals as the basic units of the ethical debate, and so contractarianism demands a particular commitment to individualism. Contractarianism is, therefore, not only a means for developing and extending ethical intuitions which have the status of conventional moralities, but is also a method of restricting the range of conventional or intuitive views which can be appropriate as the basis for a contractarian perspective.

The essential technique of contractarianism consists of asking the question: under what circumstances and under what view of rationality could a particular ethical view be argued to be the outcome of an agreement or bargain? Furthermore, are these circumstances neutral and appealing? Is the view of rationality acceptable? Can the ethical view be characterised as a reflective equilibrium? If the answers to all of these questions are satisfactory, then the ethical view under investigation is plausible and appealing.

In its most general form contractarianism may be seen as a two-stage procedure. The first stage is entirely individualistic and corresponds to the hypothetical contractarian process discussed above. Here each individual utilises his own ethical intuition and a conception of rational bargaining to reach a personal reflective equilibrium which identifies that person's own refined moral position. This position can then be thought of as informing the individual's meta-preferences, thereby revealing the link between contractarianism and the extended view of individual rationality.

The second stage of the contractarian process is then

social in nature and sees the transition from hypothetical to prospective contractarianism. The circumstances of bargaining are now shifted from the hypothetical realm to the world of real individuals, each of whom can be thought of as being in a reflective equilibrium with respect to his meta-preferences.

Just as ethical intuition and a conception of rationality form the Archimedean point for the first stage of this generalised contractarian process, so the reflective equilibria which are the outcomes of the first stage form the Archimedean point for the second stage.

The implications of this generalised form of contractarianism for the institutions of state will be taken up in Chapter 4.

I am not suggesting that this generalised contractarian method is the only means of approach to appealing ethical views, nor would I suggest that all appealing views can necessarily be approached via contractarianism.[72] In some cases a strongly intuitive view may not be amenable to being cast as a reflective equilibrium of a satisfactory bargaining game. If this is the case, it should not be taken as a decisive argument against the view. Contractarianism must be used with discretion to clarify views rather than be abused in support of, or in opposition to, any particular view. The claim is simply that contractarianism is a particularly useful tool in the context of the tension between individual rationality and substantive ethics, and in the arguments for social institutions which arise from this tension.

4 The State

4.1 ANOTHER INTRODUCTION

We are now in a position to return in more detail to the statement which opened this book. Individually rational behaviour may or may not produce collectively desirable results. If it does not, it may be possible to improve the situation by constraining individual behaviour within particular rules. These rules and their associated institutions together form a "state". The discussions of the last two chapters have explored the rich debates on rationality and collective ethics sufficiently to indicate the range of positions available and the nature of the major lines of argument; they have also provided the basis for a more detailed examination of the potential tension between these two forces and its role in the analysis of the institutions of state.

The first point to stress is the interdependence of the concepts of individual rationality and collective ethics. Rationality — whatever its particular form or content — provides the basis for ethics. In this way it is possible to say that rational individuals create their own ethical standards.

This simple point allows the identification of three varieties of tension between rationality and ethics. The first, and most extreme, is the tension of incompatibility and incoherence. If an ethical view held is grounded in a particular view of rationality, and yet a radically different view of individual rationality is held simultaneously, the resultant tensions between rationality and ethics provide no grounds for the design of institutions. Rather, the need is for a revision of the views held until they display the minimal requirement of internal consistency. An example is provided by considering the case of an ethical welfarist — perhaps a classical utilitarian — who simultaneously holds an extended view of rationality which allows for personal motivators other than utility. Such a combination of views certainly produces tensions since individually rational behaviour will not, in general, maximise welfare; and one might conceive of institutions which relieve these tensions. But such institutions would not be well grounded since the extended view of rationality, if accepted, undermines the strictly welfarist ethical position and so renders the apparent tension incoherent.

The second variety of tension is the tension of circumstance. Here the positions held on rationality and ethics are fully consistent and, moreover, harmonious in the sense that it can be demonstrated that over a broad range of relevant circumstances rational behaviour is ethically attractive. Nevertheless, there exist particular sets of circumstances which distort the normally harmonious relationship between rational action and ethically desirable action, and so generate tension. It is now possible to recognise the prisoners' dilemma as a classic example of the tension of circumstance. The original form of the prisoners' dilemma builds upon neoclassical rationality and the Paretian ethical criterion, and we have already noted the general harmony between these two views (Section 3.3).

The third variety of tension is the tension of nature. In this case the position held on individual rationality and ethics are consistent but nevertheless contain the seeds of conflict. It is not an accident of circumstance which brings the two forces into opposition, but rather the basic nature of the forces themselves. An example is provided by the combination of neoclassical rationality and liberalism. Liberalism is characterised by its insistence on the ethical precedence of individual rights, whilst neoclassical rationality recognises no individualistic obligation to respect other individuals' rights. This tension of nature arises even though liberalism can be argued to be grounded in neoclassical rationality.

A second point worthy of emphasis concerns the variety of routes by which individual rationality may impact upon the design and evaluation of institutions. So far, attention has been concentrated on just two such routes: a direct route as one of the forces held in tension to provide the justification for institutions; and an indirect route as an ingredient in the specification of the second force — the ethical criterion. There are, however, two further possible routes which must be accounted for: one concerned with the operation of institutions once established, and the second concerned with the effects of institutions on individual behaviour.

Once established, any institution will be operated by individuals; and to the extent that the design of the institution does not fully precommit the behavior of these individuals, one can expect them to behave rationally. Thus the operation of the institution will embody constrained individual rationality, where the institutional design provides the relevant constraints.

The effectiveness of an institution depends not only on its actions, but also on the reactions it stimulates. Our view of state institutions as means of influencing rational behaviour towards ethical behaviour depends upon those institutions having real effects on the behaviour of individuals. These effects must derive from the interaction between the operation of the institutions — in the forms of policies and announced rules — and individual rationality. In the final analysis, only if it is rational to respond to policy will the response occur.

The full set of routes by which rationality enters into the institutional problem is depicted in Figure 4.1 which characterises the logic of the process of institutional design. Rationality both informs this design via its role in the creation of the underlying tensions which institutions are designed to resolve, and also provides the medium through which institutions must achieve their goal. A successful institution is one which, when operated by rational individuals, will constrain rational behaviour in ethically desirable ways. In short, a successful social institution is one which uses rationality to limit itself.

Simple consistency requires that in any overall view of social institutions the same view of rationality which informs

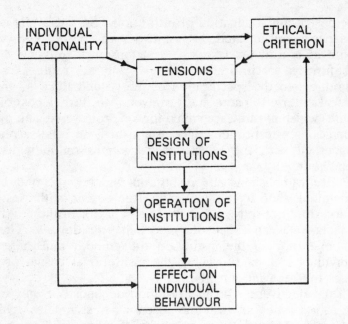

Figure 4.1: Rationality, Ethics and Institutions

the ethical criterion, and which generates tension with it, must also be used in predicting the operation and effectiveness of any institutions designed to alleviate that tension.

The discussion of Chapter 2 made possible the identification of four views of rationality which together encompassed a wide range of arguments. Each of these views of rationality may be expected to have a very different impact on the debate concerning state institutions, particularly once all four of the routes by which rationality affects institutional design are accounted for. But to complete the picture we also need to draw on Chapter 3, in which four substantive views of ethics were presented together with the contractarian procedural device which was argued to provide a means of explicitly linking a particular view of rationality to particular substantive views of ethics.

The contractarian method, together with the four views of rationality, forms the basis of the discussion of this chapter. As with earlier chapters, I will begin with the mainstream economic viewpoint. Section 4.2 and 4.3 summarise and discuss this approach first by viewing the positive analysis of the spontaneous emergence of social institutions, and subsequently by considering the very particular institutional role of government. Within the discussion of government I shall distinguish two alternative positions. The first, which might be termed the naive economic position, sees government as an essentially ethical agent; whilst the second, the "public choice" position, sees government as just another arena within which individuals pursue their rational interests. Whilst these two positions differ in many respects, they are united by their reliance upon the full neoclassical view of individual rationality.

Sections 4.4 and 4.5 will then turn to consider the implications of replacing this view of rationality with either the extended view or one of the variants of imperfect rationality. In each case I will discuss the impact on both the positive analysis of the emergence of social institutions and the nature and role of government.

The contrasts between the positions discussed in these four sections, and the range of societies which they depict, will then be emphasised in two particular areas. Section 4.6 will briefly discuss the alternative views of the relationship between the individual and the community in which he lives; Section 4.7 then discusses the role and nature of politics in each type of society.

4.2 ECONOMIC THEORY OF INSTITUTIONS

The orthodox, textbook approach to the economic analysis of institutions proceeds by modelling the institution in question — whether it be a firm, a voluntary organisation or a government agency — by direct analogy with the analysis of the individually rational decision-maker. Each institution is provided with an objective function which stands in place of individualistic preferences, and a set of constraints on behaviour which delimit a range of feasible actions. The institution then acts in the economy as if it were an agent in its own right.

Alongside this positive analysis of the behaviour of institutions stands the argument that institutions can be expected to arise whenever the situation demands them. This argument has two parts. The first concerns the spontaneous development of institutions to exploit opportunities which, for one reason or another, are unavailable to individuals. An example will clarify this possibility.

In a world of uncertainty, individuals may wish to insure themselves against fluctuations in their fortunes. However, only by pooling risks across a large number of individuals is it possible to offer effective and efficient insurance. Risk-pooling institutions such as farmers' cooperatives and insurance companies may then arise to provide this need which cannot be supplied by individuals. Clearly, this type of argument can be extended to view the formation of firms of all types,[1] and can also be utilised to view the formation of consumption clubs.[2]

The second part of the argument concerns government. In the standard or naive economic view, government is conceived as being motivated by the public interest in the sense that its objective function embodies the relevant ethical criterion — the Pareto criterion (or some particular aggregative social welfare function).

Government, in this view, acts as the supplier of institutions of last resort; establishing agencies designed to produce or facilitate actual (or potential) Pareto improvements in situations where no spontaneous private institutions emerge. This is the classic case of governmental intervention to correct market failure interpreted in institutional terms. Again an example may fix ideas.

Monopoly power implies the existence of a potential Pareto improvement and yet no private institution may emerge to reduce that power. Indeed, the only private institutions capable of such an act are potential new entrant firms which may set up in competition with the established monopoly; and there may be good technical reasons — including the behaviour of the monopolist himself — why such new entrants fail to emerge. In this setting, an authoritative governmental institution may be set up explicitly charged with the limitation of monopoly power in the public interest.

In this example, the government is acting as a policing agency, overseeing individuals and those private institutions which have emerged within society, to ensure that they do not extend their own interests to the point where they act against the public interest. But it is easy to see that an essentially similar argument could be put for the establishment of government agencies which act as positive providers of public goods not capable of being supplied by private institutions.

Government, in this view, is seen as a sort of super-institution which acts as the custodian of the public interest in both controlling society and creating new institutions wherever private institutions fail to exhaust the potential gains from organisation.[3]

This sketchy outline of the orthodox economic view clearly carries within it the contrast between rationality and ethics — with the relevant concepts being perfect neoclassical rationality and the Pareto criterion (or the weighted utilitarianism of an aggregative social welfare function). The spontaneous evolution of institutions is the direct product of individual rational behaviour, whilst the government embodies the ethical force which simultaneously restrains rationality and supplements it.

The dual role of restraint and supplementation corresponds to the distinction, made in the previous section, between two classes of tension which might arise between rationality and ethics. Tensions of circumstance are those which arise out of limitations of rationality relative to the ethical criterion, and so require supplementary institutions; whilst tensions of nature arise from rationality overreaching ethics, and so call for restraining institutions. Of course, just as the distinction between tensions of circumstance and nature may be somewhat blurred in certain cases, so the distinction between restraint and supplementation may also appear imprecise. But the general point of the dual nature of the role of government in simultaneously controlling rational behaviour and rearranging circumstances so as to encourage desirable behaviour which does not initially appear to be rational is, I think, clear enough.

Recent work in the economic theory of institutions follows the distinction between the two parts of the argument outlined above. One line of research has been concerned with the evolutionary or spontaneous emergence of institutions, and can be thought of as the development of a detailed positive economic analysis of institutional structure. The second line of work is devoted to the government aspects of the orthodox view. The main point emphasised here is that government itself is a man-made institution operated by (rational) individuals. It is therefore argued to be essentially arbitrary to assume that government acts as the protector of the public interest. This literature effectively points to our earlier identification of the four routes by which rationality conditions institutions, and points out that the orthodox view fails to take account of the route which operates via the internal process of government.

The second line of argument will be the subject of the next section, but for the remainder of this section attention will focus on the arguments concerning the evolution of institutions.

The central point in the analysis of the spontaneous evolution of institutions is that institutions arise as a direct consequence of rationality. Institutions may produce Pareto improvements and they may or may not be fully Pareto optimal, but these are unintended consequences of actions designed entirely to further individualistic ends. Since individual rationality is the cornerstone of the evolutionary approach, it is clearly appropriate to begin by viewing the evolution of self-enforcing institutions where each individual who is a party to the institution has a direct and private incentive to follow the institutional line. Self-enforcing institutions operate via norms rather than laws (Section 2.7) since there can be no question of the coercive enforcement of rules. Once the arguments concerning the spontaneous evolution of voluntary, self-enforcing institutions have been viewed, we shall turn to the possibility of the evolution of institutions based on enforcement.

It is useful to view self-enforcing institutions and their associated norms in a series of abstract cases which have formed a major presentational theme within the literature.[4] In each of the following cases each agent must choose a strategy without knowing the choice of the other, and in each case we will be interested in viewing both the one-shot game illustrated and the game involving repetitions of that basic game; we will also be concerned with the generalisation of each game to the case of more than two players.

In Table 4.1 we have a situation in which individual neoclassical rationality provides its own coordination. Strategy B is the dominant strategy for each individual and the unique equilibrium is the Pareto optimal outcome. This is true whether the game is played once or repeated; it is also clearly true if the number of players is increased. This then is the base case illustrating the underlying harmony of definition between neoclassical rationality and the Pareto criterion. The equilibrium is directly attainable and self-enforcing; no norms, laws and institutions are required. In essence the base case illustrated in Table 4.1 relates to the situation in which each individual's pay-off is independent of the action of the other agent. This independence, or lack of external effects which link the pay-offs of the one individual to the actions of another, is a key characteristic of the simple economic model of perfect competition.

Table 4.2 then introduces a pure coordination problem. In this situation neither agent has a dominant strategy, but their interests are fully coincident. As long as the two agents

Table 4.1: The Base Case

| | | Agent 2 | |
		A	B
Agent 1	A	(0,0)	(0,1)
	B	(1,0)	(1,1)

select the same strategy, a Pareto efficient equilibrium will arise which is fully self-enforcing. However, neither of these potential equilibria are directly attainable. In the one-shot game equilibrium may not be forthcoming, and in the repeated game context a stable equilibrium will only be reached and maintained through the establishment of an institutional norm. Such a norm, which merely identifies which strategy to choose, is clearly self-enforcing and can be expected to evolve in the repeated game setting. The development of such a norm is not affected by the number of players involved since each individual is acting entirely in his own interest in agreeing to the norm and his own interests are in no way diluted as the number of players increases.

Table 4.3 complicates the picture slightly by introducing a mixed-motive coordination problem.[5] In this case, as before, the agents share an interest in ensuring that they choose identical strategies, but now they have conflicting interests concerning which strategy is selected. Neither agent has a dominant strategy, but each of the two equilibria is self-enforcing since neither agent could have an incentive to change strategy unilaterally.

Table 4.2: Pure Coordination Game

		Agent 2	
		A	B
Agent 1	A	(2,2)	(0,0)
	B	(0,0)	(2,2)

Table 4.3: Mixed-motive Coordination Game

		Agent 2	
		A	B
Agent 1	A	(2,1)	(0,0)
	B	(0,0)	(1,2)

As in the previous case, the coordination problem lies in the initial establishment of an equilibrium, and this may again be overcome by an institutional norm. But now we can meaningfully distinguish alternative norms. A norm of partiality[6] is one which produces or maintains an inegalitarian equilibrium. In the context of Table 4.3, two such norms are available, one favouring each agent. In contrast, an egalitarian norm is available in the repeated game setting which effectively consists of alternating the two norms of partiality as between repetitions of the game. Each of these norms is equally effective at establishing a self-enforcing equilibrium. In the inegalitarian cases, the relatively disadvantaged agent has no credible method of disturbing the equilibrium since any action is damaging to himself. In cases of this type, therefore, whilst we may expect an institutional norm to evolve, we cannot predict its precise nature.

Table 4.4 is similar to Table 4.3 in structure and differs only in terms of the pay-off to the relatively disadvantaged agent in each of the Pareto efficient positions. But this difference is sufficient to remove the coordination aspect of the game and render the resultant game a game of conflict. Each agent has a clearly identified dominant strategy (A for agent 1, B for agent 2) so that a unique and fully rational equilibrium exists involving a pay-off of (0,0).

However, if either individual were to deviate from his dominant strategy, it would cost him nothing and provide a benefit of 2 to his counterpart. In the one-shot version of this game we could not expect a norm to emerge — the rational interests of the agents are diametrically opposed. Similarly, in the repeated game setting, we could not expect either norm of partiality to evolve since such norms can be

Table 4.4: Conflict Game

		Agent 2	
		A	B
Agent 1	A	(2,0)	(0,0)
	B	(0,0)	(0,2)

disrupted by the unilateral and costless actions of one agent. In effect, each individual has the credible threat of non-cooperation with a norm of partiality which renders such norms non-self-enforcing. This threat allows each agent to hold out for a share of the gains realised by the establishment of a norm, and in this case we may expect the egalitarian norm of alternating strategies to emerge. This egalitarian norm is fully self-enforcing since neither agent could maintain his stream of pay-offs by unilateral action in breach of the norm.

So far the cases studied have been characterised by the fact that agents faced no incentive to deviate from norm-governed behaviour once it was established. Under these circumstances self-enforcing institutions may be expected to emerge although their precise form may be unknown. Whenever a fully self-enforcing institution is available we may expect it to emerge from rationality. However, the prisoners' dilemma — reproduced as Table 4.5 — raises further issues. We have already indicated the possibility of a self-enforcing institutional solution to the repeated prisoners' dilemma, but this possibility is by no means clear-cut. In the prisoners' dilemma setting each agent always faces an incentive to act in breach of the norm. Each may argue that if he deviates from the norm just once, and then re-establishes the norm, he can be better off. Such temptations, if acted upon, would clearly lead back to the rational equilibrium pay-off of (0,0).

The temptation may be overcome, in at least some cases, by the threat of punishment or retaliation. If I expect my deviation from the norm to be punished by my counterpart refusing to re-establish the norm for some period of time,

Table 4.5: The Prisoners' Dilemma

| | | Agent 2 | |
		A	B
Agent 1	A	(1,1)	(0,2)
	B	(2,0)	(0,0)

then my incentive to deviate is diminished. Furthermore, the threat of retaliation is rational and credible since it is the only strategy available to the agent which prevents his exploitation, and so it increases the value of the stream of pay-offs. In fact, in equilibrium the threats of retaliation are never carried out, but they are not empty bluffs.

This argument is essentially similar to that used to establish the egalitarian norm in the context of Table 4.4. There, each agent had recourse to a credible threat of non-cooperation with a norm of partiality, whilst in Table 4.5 each agent has a credible threat of retaliation. The point is simply that the enforcement of the norm by such credible threats is entirely endogenous; no external agency is required. Even though the norm requires threats to ensure compliance, it is still a strictly self-enforcing norm since the relevant threats are internally generated. Such a strategy of cooperation backed by the threat of retaliation has been shown to perform well against a wide variety of alternative strategies in the context of a repeated prisoners' dilemma.[7]

Despite this argument, the private incentive to cheat on an established norm in a repeated prisoners' dilemma may still dominate. For example, the gains to cheating in the prisoners' dilemma of Table 4.6 are so large relative to the gains from norm-observing behaviour that one might expect agents to act in breach of the norm. This is particularly the case if we recall that the repeated game formulation applies when the number of repetitions of the game is unknown; so that either agent would only have to believe that there is a "reasonable" probability of the game ending within fifty repetitions to make the once and for all pay-off of 100 attractive. Under these circumstances the norm which indicates the choice of strategy A could not be expected to arise. Effectively, the punishments or threats available within the structure of the game are not sufficient to render the norm self-enforcing. Here then is the boundary between a self-enforcing norm and an externally enforced law.

If threats and punishments must lie entirely within the structure of the original game, they may be insufficient to overcome the private incentives to cheat. An obvious solution is then to import additional threats or punishments.

Table 4.6: The Incentive to Cheat

		Agent 2	
		A	B
Agent 1	A	(2,2)	(0,100)
	B	(100,0)	(1,1)

In the context of Table 4.6, if cheating could be punished by the imposition of a fine of 95, and assuming that cheating could be detected and punished costlessly, the game would be transformed into that of Table 4.7, which is still a prisoners' dilemma, but one in which the norm of selecting strategy A may be expected to emerge.

Table 4.7: The Transformed Prisoners' Dilemma

		Agent 2	
		A	B
Agent 1	A	(2,2)	(0,5)
	B	(5,0)	(1,1)

Here then we have a situation in which a self-enforcing norm may emerge as the result of the impact of an imposed, enforced law. Of course, once an external law is proposed, the punishment may be set at any required level; in particular, it may be set at a level which abolishes the prisoners' dilemma entirely. A fine of 100 would leave the pure coordination game of Table 4.8(a), where neither agent has a dominant strategy but where we would certainly expect strategy A to emerge as a norm given the perfect coincidence of interests. A fine of 100 together with a compensatory award of 2 to the exploited agent produces the game of Table 4.8(b) which is a self-coordinating game in which strategy A is the dominant strategy for each agent so that individual rationality, constrained by the law, will reach the desired outcome without the need of any further norm.[8]

Table 4.8: Transformed Games

		(a) Agent 2				(b) Agent 2	
Agent 1	A	(2,2)	(0,0)	Agent 1	A	(2,2)	(2,0)
	B	(0,0)	(1,1)		B	(0,2)	(1,1)

The question then arises: will such laws emerge spontaneously as the result of individually rational action? Will individuals effectively commit themselves to laws which restrict their own actions in exchange for a similar commitment from others?

The situation is that of Table 4.6 in which the repetition of the game is not, of itself, sufficient to induce choice of strategy A. If each agent recognises this, and recognises that it is equally true for the others, the sub-optimal, rational equilibrium will follow unless the agents can effectively precommit themselves by rendering themselves vulnerable to punishment. Here then it may be in the interest of each agent to agree to such vulnerability in advance in order to restructure the game and so open up the possibility of the norm-based solution.

The law can be conceived as deriving from prior agreement amongst the relevant parties, even though the law threatens those parties with coercive punishments. The law, in this interpretation, is precisely analogous to the rationality improving second-best strategies adopted by individuals aware of their own irrationality (Chapter 2 above). In the present context the law is rationality improving in that it enables groups of individuals to overcome tensions of circumstance which arise out of the interdependence which exists between their actions.

We may now review the status of the distinction between self-enforcing norms and enforcement laws. If both norms and laws can be expected to emerge spontaneously out of individually rational behaviour it may seem that they can be regarded as being different only as a matter of degree. Norms embody in-period mutuality of interest amongst the relevant agents, whilst laws embody the deeper ex-ante

mutuality of interests which may exist even when there are
no self-enforcing equilibria. Another way of viewing this
distinction is that norms arise from mutuality of interests
within the game, whilst laws arise from mutuality of interests
concerning transformations of the game.

However, the temptation to reunite norms and laws under
the banner of spontaneously emerging institutions is potentially misleading. Once the costs of bargaining are accounted
for, a sharp distinction between norms and laws re-emerges.
The basic point here is most clearly seen in many-person
games where the incentive to precommit for any individual
may be severely diluted. This problem can be thought of as
a form of potentially infinite regress of prisoners' dilemmas
each with its own incentive to free-ride. The game itself is
the first-level prisoners' dilemma, but the bargain concerning the institution of a law may form a second-level
prisoners' dilemma in which each individual's most preferred position is that all others bind themselves with law
whilst he remains unbound. This problem will be particularly apparent in large groups where the possibility of
free-riding is more apparent.[9]

It may be objected that each agent — even in a large
group setting — will eventually come to see that the mutual
advantage of all lies in agreement to the law and, ultimately,
in the cooperative strategy; and that the eventual or perfect
bargaining outcome will therefore entail this agreement.
However, there are two faults with this objection. At the
practical level it is of little interest what any "perfect bargaining outcome" may be; it is sufficient to point out that
just as there may be no self-enforcing equilibrium in the
first-level prisoners' dilemma, so there may be no self-
enforcing or accessible resolution to the second-level prisoners' dilemma. A viable route to the law may not exist.

The second fault lies at the more abstract level where it
may be suggested that the very concept of a "perfect bar-
ganing outcome" is ill-defined. Bargaining between individuals proceeds only by compromise and concession, and
individuals will only rationally concede if there is some cost
to the continuation of bargaining. If one abstracts from
bargaining costs one loses all of the force for resolution

which exists within bargaining situations. On the other hand, once bargaining costs are explicitly recognised — as they must be — one cannot sensibly appeal to any specific notion of a perfect bargaining outcome. Bargaining outcomes will depend on the various perceptions of bargaining costs, and will typically be neither "perfect" nor uniquely identifiable.

In some situations genuine laws may emerge voluntarily and spontaneously, but there can be no guarantee of this since their emergence depends upon a costly and imperfect process and may involve a sucession of higher-order prisoners' dilemmas. This is in sharp contrast to self-enforcing norms which emerge without the need for higher-level bargaining.

Thus far, our discussion of the emergence of institutions has been almost entirely positive. It is now time to return briefly to the normative questions of whether spontaneously emergent institutions are necessarily justified, and whether any institution which does not emerge voluntarily can be ethically justified, before taking up the topic of government in the next section.

The mainstream economic answer to these questions is determined by reference to the Paretian criterion (or the weighted utilitarian criterion) interpreted as an exogenously given yardstick. Spontaneously emerging institutions are Pareto approved provided that the group over which the institution is defined to be self-enforcing includes all those affected by the institution. However, since Olson (1965), it has been commonplace to argue that the institutions most likely to emerge spontaneously are those based on a narrowly defined group with a clearly defined common interest which can be pursued at the expense of some broader, more heterogeneous and weaker group. Such narrow special-interest organisations or institutions which may emerge directly from individual rationality will not pass the Pareto criterion.

Equally, the Pareto criterion may approve of institutions which are inaccessible to individual rationality and which will not, therefore, emerge spontaneously. In these ways, spontaneous emergence is neither a necessary nor a sufficient condition for ethical justification, in the main-stream economic view.

The contractarian viewpoint is useful in establishing the ethical status of institutions since, as a procedural theory of ethical justification, it can be applied directly without the need to refer to any abstract ethical criterion which might be viewed as the outcome of the contractarian process in any particular formulation. Spontaneously emerging institutions are clearly the product of real agreements or "contracts" and superficially this might seem to imply that the contractarian method must approve of them. However, our discussion of contractarianism stressed the point that contractarianism carries ethical or justificatory force only to the extent that the original bargaining or choice-situation is considered to be appropriate. Thus, in analysing the justification of any institution which actually emerges, the contractarian would focus attention on the nature of the situation from which the institution emerged — if this situation has the desirable characteristics of an Archimedean point, then and only then, would the resultant institution be approved.

This is the contractarian method applied to the evaluation of extant institutions, but a variant of the same method is applicable to the evaluation of novel institutions. Here the basic question to be asked is — could the proposed insti-tution have been chosen by rational individuals at an Arch-imedean point? The mere fact that the institution has not emerged is not evidence in favour of a negative answer to this question. Non-emergence may result from the non-Archimedean nature of the actual bargaining situation, or it may simply arise from the natural limitations of the pro-cess of bargaining. Just as the mere existence of an agree-ment does not imply a contractarian justification, so the absence of an actual agreement does not imply the absence of contractarian justification.

4.3   EFFECTIVE INSTITUTIONS

Alternative substantive ethical theories will provide diff-ering views on the appropriate restraints to be placed on spontaneously emerging institutions, and on the desirability of supplementing the set of institutions. However, to become operational each ethical theory requires a means by which such restraint and supplementation can be pursued; this means is government.

As I have already noted, the orthodox economic approach to government is simply to assume that it operates as if motivated in the public interest. this view of government as an essentially ethical agent is independent of any particular conception of the public interest. Government may be viewed as an impersonal, ethical *deus ex machina* regardless of whether the particular criterion it applies is Paretian, utilitarian, libertarian or whatever.

But government itself is an institution operating via particular processes and the actions of individuals. To assume that government acts in the public interest, and then to define the public interest exogenously, is to undermine both the analysis of government as an effective institution and the analysis of the justification of government.

The spontaneously emerging institutions discussed in the previous section are effective (though not necessarily justified) institutions since they are predicated on the rational behaviour of all individuals party to the institution. The institution is not represented as a separate entity modelled as having objectives of its own, but rather as a set of procedural rules which constrain or supplement the actions of individuals. We have seen that such effective institutions may arise directly out of individual rationality, and that their ethical justification can be investigated by reference to the contractarian method.

These same comments can be made in relation to government. If government is to be treated endogenously as an institution to be justified, if must be analysed as an effective institution which operates to influence individual action by means of policies which emerge from the actions of individuals within a framework of procedural rules. The analysis must proceed not by analogy with individual rationality with government placed in the position of a supreme agent, but by application of individual rationality with government seen as a particular setting within which individual rationality is made effective.

This approach to government, based directly on individual rationality in the neoclassical sense, has developed into a sub-discipline within economics over the past thirty-five years.[10] The Downs model of representative democracy is built on the notion that political representatives, coalitions and parties select their policy platforms in order to maximise the probability of election to power. This basic hypothesis of self-interest allows for the derivation of a large number of predictions ranging from those concerning the strategic positioning of political parties in a multi-party system, to "Director's Law" — which argues that redistribution towards the middle of the income distribution and away from both the rich and the poor can be expected to follow from such rational politics — and to the importance of log-rolling and lobbying in ensuring that special-interest legislation is more likely to reach the statute book than general-interest legislation.

Breton (1974) extends this view of government by use of an analogy with an industrial monopolist. The incumbent government is seen as a monopoly agency which can be expected to exploit its position of power subject only to the constraints acting upon it. These constraints are of three basic types. The threat of new entry is the standard constraint on monopoly in the market setting, and in the governmental context this constraint can be interpreted as an electoral restriction; the threat of rejection at the next election may limit the government's abuse of power in the present in order that it may retain power and so increase the long-term total benefit.

A second category of constraint is emphasised by Niskanen (1971) who distinguishes between the politician and the bureaucrat and argues that the rational bureaucrat will seek to maximise the budget allocation to his bureau in order to maximise the prospects for promotion, increased status and so on. The actions of the bureacrat, in this view, will not be simply to carry out the instructions of his political master, but to interpret those instructions in the manner most advantageous to the bureau and so promote his own interests whilst constraining the actions of government. The inertia of the civil service is a symptom not of inefficiency but rather of the rational action of bureaucrats in protecting their own position, which has as an unintended consequence the limitation of the discretionary, monopoly power of government.

The third category of constraints acting on government is that of institutional structure which may be embedded in a constitution which may also explicitly delimit governmental authority.[11] These constitutional constraints act on government to hold a referendum on each and every issue, and to other institutions and individuals; they provide a framework of rules, requirements and prohibitions which, at least as a first approximation, can be regarded as fixed.

In this setting, government *per se* carries with it no particular ethical authority unless it is embodied in the constitution. If a government motivated by the neoclassical rationality of its individual members were not constitutionally constrained there could be no presumption that governmental action would constrain or supplement the actions of private individuals or spontaneously emergent institutions in a manner consistent with any particular ethical view. Thus, whereas the orthodox economic view places ethical responsibility directly with the government, the "public choice" perspective uses the analysis of government as an institution of rationality to shift attention one stage backwards on to the constitution as the source of ethical authority within society.

At first sight this might look like the first step in a potentially infinite regress, with each step investing ethical authority in the rules which govern the process for choosing the rules which govern the process . . . . Landes and Posner (1975) attempt to take the next step on this route by arguing that the constitution — whether a formal written code or an informal set of inherited conventions — is the product of self-interested rational choice by particular interest groups, and so carries no particular ethical significance. However, there is an argument for cutting off this potential infinite regress at the constitutional level; this argument depends upon the contractarian method.

The contractarian argument endows a constitution with ethical authority if and only if it can be viewed as the

outcome of rational agreement originating in an Archimedean point. Such a constitution then controls government to at least some degree. Of course, contractarianism
could be used simply to evaluate government actions, but
this would provide no control over those actions which
emerge from rationality. The constitution, in the contractarian interpretation, transforms ethical evaluation into
ethical control, and the infinite regress is avoided by appeal
to the Archimedean nature of the contractarian process
used to specify the constitution.

In this view the constitution embodies ethical authority
which operates via constraints and requirements on government which, in turn, imposes constraints and requirements
on the actions of private individuals and emergent institutions. But it is important to note that government is not
only constrained and obliged by the constitution, it is also
justified by it.

The question of how effective ethical authority can be if
it operates only by this rather indirect route is a very real
one. By its nature, a constitution is intended to cover a
multitude of situations which cannot be predicted *a priori*;
under these circumstances a constitution cannot hope either
to prescribe or to proscribe particular governmental actions
except in relatively extreme cases. This implies that the
major impact of a constitution must be felt in its deter-
mination of the processes by which in-period governmental
decisions are made.[12]

This emphasis on the constitutional control of procedures
rather than outcomes goes far beyond the specification of
the method of selecting our electing governments from time
to time. Decision-making procedures within parliaments,
government departments, ministries and cabinets all provide
systems of checks and balances on governmental discretion;
as do constitutional provisions which establish an independent judiciary, a separation of powers between distinct
legislative bodies, a tier of local government independent
of central government, and so on. But even allowing for
the full range of procedural controls, a constitution drawn
up in a state of considerable uncertainty regarding the future

situations in which it must operate could not hope to do more than influence governmental action to lie within fairly broad limits. Certainly such a constitution could not guarantee that governmental actions were always consistent with some guiding ethical criterion; still less could it be claimed that governmental actions were optimal with respect to that criterion.

It might be objected that government discretion can be eliminated completely by imposing constitutional rules which fully determine outcomes by specifying strict procedures. For example, a constitution might require government to hold a referendum on each and every issue, and to implement the decision of that referendum whatever it might be. However, even leaving aside considerations of cost which would be relevant at the constitutional level (Buchanan and Tullock, 1962), there can be no general presumption that constraints of this fully-binding variety would advance the cause of the particular ethical criterion. The purpose of the constitution is not to constrain government discretion *per se*, but to promote ethically desirable action by selective imposition of checks and balances. In the unlikely event that a fully procedurally binding constitution was ethically desirable it could, of course, be expected to emerge from the contractarian analysis, so that no separate treatment of this case is warranted.

The overall picture of a society driven by perfect neoclassical rationality and seen through contractarian eyes might be sketched as follows. A relevant ethical criterion could be established by the contractarian method, using the appropriate concept of rationality and an acceptable description of an Archimedean point. It is clear from our earlier discussions of contractarianism, and in particular the works of Rawls, Nozick and Roemer, that a relatively broad range of ethical positions ranging from libertarian to Marxian may be derived from this exercise depending upon the precise formulation of the Archimedean point. Furthermore, if individuals in this fully neoclassical world have no ethical or moral intuitions or conventions — so that they are strictly *homo economicus* responding only to self-interested rationality — there can be no appeal to the notion of reflective equilibrium, which might help to narrow down the range of allowable ethical positions.

However, the precise nature of the ethical position which would emerge from the contractarian method is of limited operational importance, since the only means of rendering the ethical criterion forceful is via a set of constitutional rules which serve both to justify and to restrain an authoritative government. But, as we have seen, the constitution will not in general fully bind government to act in accordance with the underlying ethical principle. The constitution, by its nature, will allow government considerable in-period discretion, and in this neoclassical world government can be expected to exploit this discretion to further its own rational ends.

Government actions to restrain or supplement the actions of private individuals and emergent institutions are therefore produced out of rationality constrained to some degree by an ethically justified constitution where the underlying ethic is itself — at another level — derived from rationality.

The ethical authority in such a society is weak, but nevertheless it is sufficient to justify government, since even the weakly constrained government will improve the social situation relative to the position in which no authority has dominion over in-period rationality. Indeed, such a society may be argued to be ethically superior to the Hobbesian formulation of civil society in which a completely unconstrained sovereign is argued to be preferred to the anarchy of individual rationality. This assertion clearly depends upon the constitutional constraints being justified in contractarian terms. There can obviously be no general claim that arbitrary constraints on rational government are ethically justified.

The tension between individual rationality and ethics in this neoclassical world of *homo economicus* pulls heavily in favour of rationality. It is hardly surprising that in a world in which no one recognises any ethical or moral obligation at the individual level, and where no ethical intuitions or commitments are available to ground the contractarian process, society can be only weakly constrained by ethics — even where the ethic is endogeneously determined.

This picture of the neoclassically rational society is not, I think, a true likeness to actual society although it contains many resemblances. The criticisms of neoclassical rationality put in Chapter 2 carry over with considerable weight as criticisms of this model of society. In the next two sections we shall investigate the impact of respecifying the content of the notion of rationality as the view of institutions, government, constitutions and their ethical justification.

4.4 INSTITUTIONS AND EXTENDED RATIONALITY

Two principal features of the extended view of rationality discussed in Chapter 2 provide the starting point for our investigation of its implications for the institutional structure of society. The first is the conception of the individual in terms of a range of "preference functions" each of which represents one aspect of the individual or one level of commitment. This conception carries with it the clear possibility of a tension between commitments within the individual which resembles in at least some respects the tension between individual rationality and collective ethics.

The second important feature of the approach is that it admits moral or ethical commitments and obligations at the purely individualistic level. Indeed, Sen's notion of a meta-preference is explicitly an ethical formulation.[13] Such personal ethical intuitions or conventions provide the basis for the operation of the generalised contractarian method at the individualistic level. Hypothetical contractarianism is then capable of locating, for each individual, a reflective equilibrium deriving from an ethically significant Archimedean point.

In a world of extended rationality we may still distinguish between the positive analysis of institutions or norms which may emerge out of individual rationality, and the normative discussion of the ethical authority of institutions in general and the institution of government in particular.

In terms of the positive analysis, the range of institutions which can be expected to evolve spontaneously out of extended rationality differs from that associated with neoclassical rationality in one major respect. I have already suggested (Section 2.7) that the extended view of rationality lends itself to the possibility that individuals may erect institutional devices as a means of diffusing the internal tension between alternative commitments: effectively, as a means of externally policing self-control. Groups of individuals who share a particular commitment can be expected to externalise their common concern in the form of an explicit institutional arrangement. Examples which might be more difficult to explain on the alternative hypotheses of purely neoclassical rationality are provided by charitable organisations which may be interpreted as acting as focal points for particular altruistic commitments (Section 2.5).

However, just as the institutions which evolve directly from purely neoclassical rationality do not necessarily carry any ethical justification, so the more extensive range of institutions which can be expected to emerge spontaneously in a world of extended rationality cannot automatically lay claim to justification. The ethical authority which, in the extended view of rationality, can be grounded in individual commitments still requires an institutional mechanism to render it operational at the social level.

The hypothetical contractarian argument, together with an individual's basic moral commitment or meta-preference, can provide each individual with an ethical view on a social scale which satisfies the condition of a reflective equilibrium. Each individual has an internally consistent view of the good society, and can derive from this a constitution which forms the basis for government leading towards that society.

It is important to note that the power of the constitution and, therefore, the operational power of the ethical force, is more extensive in this setting than was the case in the world of neoclassical rationality. Because individuals are not motivated entirely by self-interest, it is possible to appeal to the spirit of the constitution as well as the letter. As was suggested in Section 2.17, the individual characterised by extended rationality will have some respect for rules *qua* rules, and this respect increases the potential effectiveness of constitutional rules. This point applies both at the governmental level (where the politician will view the constitution not only as constraint but also as guideline) and at the more general individual level where individuals may accept, as part of their commitment, the value of any particular government act even though it is contrary to their own self-interest.

Yet, the specifically personal view of the good society produced by the hypothetical contractarian argument still leaves open the question of the transition from the individual level to the social. Here we move from the realms of hypothetical contractarianism to the more concrete ground of prospective contractarianism (Sections 3.5, 3.9). Actual bargaining between real individuals, each in a state of reflective equilibrium, characterises this second stage of the ethical process. Whilst the individual's ethical intuition or convention provides the Archimedean point for the hypothetical contractarianism of the first stage, the reflective equilibrium of that first stage provides the Archimedean point for the second.

We may distinguish two broad classes of outcomes to this two-stage ethical process informed by extended rationality — the Utopian and the pluralist. Each will be discussed in turn.

Utopian solutions to the ethical process can be characterised as those which arise when the prospective contract stage of the process involves a trivial or degenerate bargain amongst individuals. In other words, Utopian solutions are those which arise when all individuals share the same reflective equilibrium as a result of the first, hypothetical contract, stage of the process. In these circumstances there is complete mutuality of interest and immediate unanimity on the ethical criterion relevant to society and, therefore, on the institutional and constitutional structure appropriate to that society. Utopia, by this definition, is any society in which there is complete agreement on all ethical questions.[14]

A Utopian outcome does not require that all individuals

are substantially identical, only that they become effectively identical at the end of the first stage of the ethical process. People may begin with widely varying ethical conventions, but a Utopian solution may still emerge if these differing conventions converge to a particular reflective equilibrium as a result of the hypothetical contractarian process.

The set of Utopian solutions is, of course, large: as large as the set of individualistic reflective equilibria. Each substantive ethical theory provides a possible reflective equilibrium and hence a possible Utopia. From the contractarian viewpoint each possible Utopia shares the characteristic that the underlying ethical criterion, the constitution, and hence the governmental process, derives directly from unanimous consent. It is clear that, in the presence of such consent, the constitutional government can claim full authority in the sense that the individuals in society have all precommitted themselves to the strategy of obedience to constitutional rule. In this sense it is the precommitment of obligation which is the source of authority. This argument for authority grounded in unanimous consent is basic to many views of political authority.[15]

In order to explore the nature of the class of Utopias implied by unanimity amongst individuals of extended rationality, it is useful to rehearse the argument against the proposition that all consensual Utopias must converge to anarchism. The outline of the argument for this proposition is that if government authority is predicated on unanimous acceptance of obligation, that authority is not real, since it can never be used to coerce. Thus, government in Utopia is argued to be merely a convenient fiction which serves to obscure the underlying anarchism.

The argument against this anarchist proposition may be put in two parts, the first concerned with the individual, the second with the community. First, because of the nature of extended rationality, the government in Utopia may have a real and significant role in operating to constrain (or promote) certain aspects of individual behaviour which the individual would himself wish constrained (or promoted). This is the distinction between the individual's ability to precommit his actions by purely internal techniques, and his ability to precommit by use of the external device of government. The second method may simply be more effective and so provide a real role for government in Utopia.

The second part of the argument concerns tensions of circumstance such as the prisoners' dilemma. Depending upon the particular nature of a given Utopia, it may be the case that the individualistic commitment, when translated into the collective ethic, is revealed to be collectively self-defeating so that no entirely self-enforcing, ethically acceptable outcome can be guaranteed. In such circumstances it is entirely rational for the individuals voluntarily and unanimously to agree to establish a government empowered to enforce the ethical solution. This is, in effect, the possibility of the spontaneous emergence of a law (as opposed to a norm) which was discussed in Section 4.2.

This second part of the argument can be reinforced and renterpreted in the light of Taylor's (1982) discussion of anarchism. Taylor's major thesis, expressed in our terminology, is that anarchy can survive in certain societies, in contradiction to Nozick's argument concerning the inevitability of the evolution of the night-watchman government, once pure neoclassical rationality is replaced with a broader conception of rationality. More particularly, Taylor identifies three fundamental properties of "community" which are necessary for the support of anarchism.[16] The first property is that all members of the community should share some set of common beliefs and values. Our Utopian societies clearly exhibit this characteristic in the extreme form of complete agreement on all ethical questions. Thus far then the set of Utopias is consistent with anarchy.

Taylor's second property is that the members of the community should have direct and many-sided relationships with each other. This is taken to limit the size of anarchic communities by an argument similar to Olson's argument directed at the spontaneous creation of interest groups.[17] In our present context we have said nothing about the size of Utopian societies. The Olson–Taylor argument suggests that Utopias can only be anarchistic if they are sufficiently "small".

The third property identified by Taylor as being a necessary precondition for anarchy is a degree of reciprocity, cooperation or altruism in inter-personal relations. It is this feature of Taylor's schema which relates to the prisoners' dilemma and, more generally, to tensions of circumstance. If individuals' commitments (and therefore their reflective equilibrium, and therefore their ethic) include a degree of altruism of the type required to transform a prisoners' dilemma into an assurance game (Section 2.6), then the Utopia associated with that ethic may be of the type capable of supporting anarchy. However, many reflective equilibria do not include such altruism or reciprocity, so many Utopias do not conform to the conditions which, in Taylor's argument, are required to render anarchy feasible.

Utopias in which the number of individuals is small, and where the underlying ethic incorporates a particular commitment to altruism, may be anarchistic.[18] But it is clear that not all Utopias satisfy these conditions. In some Utopias, at least, constitutional government is not merely fictional but actually serves a purpose in operationalising individual desires — expressed unanimously — at the social level.

One final general point concerning Utopian solutions to the ethical process may be made before turning to consider pluralist solutions. It is in the nature of Utopias that the government has a clear and well-specified criterion by which to evaluate its actions and by which to make all policy decisions. Furthermore, the individuals who populate government offices accept and indeed actively agree with this criterion so that there is no conflict between the motivation of the office and the motivation of the office holder. Clearly then, politics in Utopia is essentially simple. This is not to deny that, in particular cases, it may be difficult to actually perform the calculations necessary to reach a decision between alternative courses of actions. Uncertainty and the nature of the network of social effects occasioned by any governmental action may make decision-making difficult in this purely computational sense. But it is never complex in the sense that there can be no deep disagreements on policy other than on empirical grounds. Another way of indicating this essential simplicity is to point out that Utopias, whatever their particular substantive ethic might be, are effectively one-party states.

Pluralist solutions to the ethical process arise whenever there is genuine bargaining at the second, prospective contractarian, stage of the process — in other words, whenever the individualistic reflective equilibria which result from the first stage of the process differ between individuals so that there can be no direct or immediate unanimity on the ethical criterion relevant to society or, therefore, on the institutional and constitutional structure appropriate to that society. Pluralist societies, by this definition, are those in which there are deep disagreements on ethical questions.[19]

The simple fact of basic disagreement does not, of course, rule out the possibility of a bargaining outcome which is unanimously approved. The implication is simply that the second state of prospective bargaining is substantial in pluralist societies whereas in Utopias it is trivial. The fundamental question in pluralist societies then concerns the nature of the agreement than can be reached on the basis of individualistic ethical views which are deeply divergent.

Clearly no concrete answer can be given to this question unless the precise range of ethical views relevant to the bargaining situation is specified, and even then the range of possible bargaining outcomes may be large. No attempt to classify particular bargaining outcomes will, therefore, be made. Rather, I shall concentrate on just one or two simple points which can be expected to carry weight in any pluralist bargain, and which are suggested by the contractarian method.

Our emphasis on the role of individual rationality in grounding ethical values makes it clear that individualism, in a very particular form, must play a very special role in our discussion. The recognition of individuals as the ultimate source of values provides the particular form of individualism of crucial importance.[20]

Individualism of this form is also fundamental to the generalised contractarian method presented here since, as we have already noted, the contractarian process not only refines ethical intuitions or conventions, but also delimits the range of ethical intuitions which may provide a starting point for the process. A respect for individualism, in the sense that each individual recognises the ultimate importance of individualistic commitments, and the resultant authority of agreement amongst individuals at the hypothetical level and, therefore, the prospective level, is a necessary ingredient of contractarianism.

Strictly, then, we are concerned with the analysis of the emergence of society out of agreement amongst people who share this basic form of individualism. That individuals intent on forming a society should have some degree of common ground is hardly controversial,[21] but the restriction to individualism may sound severe. However, the particular form of individualism required is much less restrictive than it may at first appear.

Our individuals may include some — indeed any number — whose personal reflective equilibrium is substantially anti-individualist. Their personal ethical viewpoint may be entirely socialist or communitarian in content and implication. Such anti-individualism in the outcome of the ethical process is perfectly consistent with our analysis provided that these reflective equilibria can be derived on the individualistic basis of the personal hypothetical contract. It is individualism in the form of the ethical argument, rather than individualism in the substantive content of the derived ethic, which is of importance.

Given such basic, formal individualism, the prospective stage of the contractarian process must be characterised as an arena for agreement between individuals who may differ in terms of ethical views, but who are otherwise equal. Tolerance then becomes the common denominator of the prospective contract in pluralist settings: tolerance of individual differences not only in interests or tastes but also in ethical values. As a minimum, such tolerance can be expected to result in a constitutional requirement of what Gordon refers to as "political pluralism": "the doctrine that, since individuals differ in their values and their interests, collective decisions should be made by procedures which permit participation by all members of society" (Gordon, 1980, p. 47).

Gordon goes on to argue that the decentralisation of political power and the opportunity to participate in the political process in a variety of ways will also be constitutional devices of value in a pluralist society.

This prescription of constitutional rules to embody tolerance is strikingly similar to that discussed above in relation to the purely neoclassical world. There, participation and decentralisation were to limit the monopoly power of government, whereas in the present context the same constitutional provisions are argued to operationalise tolerance by giving each distinct ethical view a voice in the decision-making process, and by attempting to prevent all government power from falling into the possession of a particular ethically motivated group. In the fully neoclassical setting, constitutional restraints of this kind were argued to provide only weak ethical control, but in the present context this point is not directly relevant since the purpose of the constitutional control is not the furtherance of some particular ethical view but the tolerance of all ethical views. Thus, constitutional controls of this kind can be argued to be much more effective in the context of extended rationality in a pluralist society.

However, participation and decentralisation do not, in themselves, offer any assurance of individual respect in the outcomes of the social decision-making process, and we might view the stronger possibility of designing institutions and constitutions which incorporate the notion of respect into government outcomes as well as the governmental process.

Gordon notes that in a pluralist society political problems cannot be solved in the simple, computational sense. In contrast to our description of Utopia, politics in pluralist societies is essentially complex. Indeed, it may be argued (Section 4.7) that politics in this setting is the art of the impossible. The ability to make decisions in the absence of a criterion — or, more accurately, the presence of an abundance of alternative criteria each carrying the firm commitment of a section of the community — lies at the very heart of pluralist society.

One way of gaining some leverage on this political problem is by accounting for the impact of alternative decisions on the cohesiveness of society itself, and it is here that the notion of respect for individuals and their values can be incorporated into governmental outcomes. If respect for individuals is basic to society, social cohesion can be maintained or increased by ensuring that political outcomes do not alienate particular groups within society by consistently affronting their firmly held values. In this way, one role for government in a pluralist society is to ensure that alternative, and perhaps mutually inconsistent, ethical values are sustained — one might even say cherished — within society. Government in a pluralist society has to be decisive in the face of alternative values, but decisive in a way that ensures the continuation of a pluralist society, that transforms conflict into tolerance, preserves heterogeneity and binds together various groups rather than divides them.

This view of a "moral society" predicated on moral diversity and devoted to sustaining that diversity is explored by Calabresi and Bobbitt in their discussion of the "tragic choices" which arise in the context of heterogeneous values.[22] They argue that different decision-making rules will tend to produce outcomes which threaten different values and that in order to preserve and cherish all values society will need, from time to time, to vary its decision-making procedures. Effectively they suggest that society should periodically reorder its own power structure in order to preserve a variety of ideals and produce a greater social cohesion in the long run. Pluralist society, in this view, is a dynamic society in which there is no optimal set of decision-making procedures, and no optimal static constitution, but a continuing need for reform and change directed not at some ultimate Utopia but simply at the preservation of variety.

The notions of tolerance and respect in a pluralist society require some further elaboration in order to view the claim that variety in social institutions and decision-making procedures may be characteristic elements of pluralist agreements.

At the prospective stage of bargaining, agents face each other from distinct ethical positions and attempt to agree on ethical questions and, in particular, the form of the constitution which will provide ethical authority for government in their society. Given the fundamental divergence in the ethical criteria held we may identify three possible types of outcome. The first is failure. It may be the case that each agent's own ethical conviction is such that anarchistic autonomy is preferable to any available society which, perforce, will include individuals with other ethical views. This is the extreme of intolerance where the Utopian demand for ethical purity makes society and community impossible.

A second possibility is compromise. Under certain circumstances, one can imagine a solution to the prospective bargain which elevates one particular ethical viewpoint to the status of the agreed ethic, with each individual trading off his own ethical commitments against the gains from association. If such a society came about it would, in our definition, be a *de facto* Utopia since a unique ethical viewpoint should be established as the socially relevant ethic with all individuals agreeing to this establishment.

However, it is unlikely that such a compromise solution would arise. Whilst it is certainly eminently possible to imagine ethical compromises on some specific issues, it is not the case that ethical criteria themselves may be compromised in this way, since this would require some higher-order criterion by which to evaluate the trade-off between ethics and the gains of association.[23] Compromise will have an important role to play in pluralist societies but it cannot be expected to resolve the fundamental problem.

The third possibility is tolerance. Here each individual recognises the validity of the other's ethical viewpoint whilst disagreeing with its content. Tolerance is then the explicit agreement to disagree, and the structuring of social institutions to operationalise this agreement which respects alternative and contrary viewpoints.

Within such a framework, the possibility of variation in institutional structures and decision-making procedures is similar to the use of alternating norms in certain game situations.[24] In the game context, alternation of different strategies provides incentives to all individuals to maintain a self-enforcing norm, and the analogy carries over directly to pluralist society where a constitutional strategy of alternation may be an effective means of providing each ethical group with incentives to participate in society.

In any given version of Utopia, whether it is that of Rawls or Nozick or some other, the appropriate constitutional and institutional structure of society is, at least conceptually, well defined. The unique ethical criterion which lies at the heart of all Utopias provides an unfailing guide. In pluralist societies no such simple image of the optimal institutional arrangement can be held. Constitutions and institutions are still of very considerable importance, but their value is not directed towards a well-specified target, but rather is directed towards maintaining the coordinate existence of a number of alternative targets.

The ethical force is strong and unidirectional in any Utopia and it carries sufficient force to override individual rationality whenever the two are held in tension, precisely because the Utopian ideal is grounded in individualistic unanimity. In Utopia the collective ethic always dominates the individual, but in some versions of Utopia the relevant collective ethic explicitly reinstates the individual as an ethical agent.

In the case of pluralist societies there is no unidirectional ethical force, and the tension between individual rationality and *the* ethic is translated into a tension between alternative individualistic conceptions of ethics. I have suggested that this tension must be maintained, indeed cherished, rather than resolved if the society is to be preserved. The institutional framework which permits such maintenance of tension is that associated with open government and the absence of firmly entrenched and long-established power groups. The continuous and often cyclical reform of societal institutions may appear, from the point of view of the orthodox economists, to be evidence of inefficiency at best and intransitivity and hence irrationality at worst; but in this argument such reform, and cycles in political and institutional life, may be the very embodiment of ethical pluralism based on the extended notion of individual rationality.

4.5 INSTITUTIONS AND IMPERFECT RATIONALITY

The essential feature of imperfect rationality is the individual's self-recognition of his limitation, and his consequent search for second-best, rationality-improving stratagems, usually involving precommitment. These stratagems may be entirely internal to the individual, but it is more likely that they involve external arrangements, and these may well be institutional in form. This argument concerning the use of external institutional devices for precommitment is similar to that employed in the case of perfect extended rationality, where the internal tension arose between alternative levels of commitment within the individual.

There is, therefore, a presumption in favour of the view that the introduction of imperfect rationality may produce an individualistic demand for governmental action in the provision of institutions which would have no value in a world of perfect rationality. However, a theory of imperfect rationality is only fully defined relative to a particular theory of perfect rationality; in what follows, therefore, we must distinguish between imperfect neoclassical rationality and imperfect extended rationality.

In the positive analysis of the evolution of institutions, the first and most basic point is that the set of institutions which emerges under imperfect rationality may be expected to differ from that which emerges under the relevant notion of perfect rationality. Imperfect rationality will encourage some institutions to emerge which would not emerge under perfect rationality, whilst simultaneously preventing the emergence of some institutions which would evolve under perfect rationality.

The possibility that imperfect neoclassical rationality might give rise to institutions not necessarily accessible to perfectly neoclassical rational individuals was illustrated in Section 2.4 where it was argued that a population of imperfectly rational individuals who had adopted satisficing as a second-best strategy might reach stable collective agreements in a situation which would be recognised as a prisoners' dilemma by any perfectly neoclassical rational individual. A similar example could easily be constructed for the case of imperfect extended rationality.

This example was arranged to show that an imperfection in rationality might lead to an improvement in the eventual outcome as judged by any particular ethical criterion; but there can be no guarantee that all institutions which emerge from imperfect rationality share this ethical justification.

A second class of institutions which may emerge spontaneously under imperfect rationality, but not under perfect rationality, are those mentioned above which simply act as external devices for precommitment. Such institutions are rationality improving by nature but this, again, does not imply any ethical justification.

The posssibility that perfectly rational institutions might fail to emerge under imperfect rationality is even more apparent. It is in the nature of imperfect rationality — whether neoclassical or extended — that individuals misperceive their own rational interests. It is therefore possible that such individuals will simply fail to recognise the value of potential institutional arrangements. Such simple misperception also provides a third argument for the emergence of institutions under imperfect rationality which would not evolve in the context of perfect rationality.

The position may be summarised by noting that the impact of the introduction of imperfect rationality on the evolution of institutions can be broken down into predictable and unpredictable elements. The predictable element consists of the argument concerning external devices for precommitment, and this implies that imperfect rationality may support a broader range of emergent institutions than the relevant notion of perfect rationality. The unpredictable element which overlays this effect corresponds to the relative under- and over-supply of institutions on the grounds of misperception and the avoidance of prisoners' dilemmas. This unpredictable element makes it impossible to conclude whether any particular institution which would emerge as a self-enforcing norm under a particular concept of perfect rationality, will in fact emerge under the related notion of imperfect rationality. This in turn opens up the possibility that some institutions, if introduced exogenously into an imperfectly rational world, might prove to be self-enforcing once they are recognised by the relevant individuals. We shall return to this point shortly.

I have already argued (Section 3.8) that in constructing the contractarian argument concerning the normative justification of institutions, the distinction between perfect and imperfect rationality is of little significance. Since the imperfectly rational individual recognises his irrationality, it seems clear that in searching for a reflective equilibrium he would specify perfect rationality (of the appropriate form) as a condition of the Archimedean point.

By this argument, the introduction of imperfect rationality can do nothing to strengthen, or in any way alter, ethical authority and its constitutional impact in a world of neoclassical rationality. Neither can imperfect rationality change the nature of the first stage of the ethical process in a world of extended rationality. The second — prospective contractarian — stage of the process may be affected to the extent that it consists of actual, non-trivial bargaining. In a Utopian world where no real bargaining is either required or possible, the step from the shared reflective equilibrium to the unique social ethic is immediate and requires no appeal to rationality. Imperfect rationality, therefore, cannot impinge on Utopia by this route. However, in pluralist society where real bargaining is required at the second stage of the contractarian process, imperfectly rational individuals may be expected to reach different outcomes from those associated with perfect extended rationality displaying the same range of commitments and the same range of reflective equilibria. Imperfect rationality, therefore, can be expected to influence the detailed constitutional and institutional evaluations in a pluralist society. However, I have already suggested that the major characteristics of pluralist bargains are largely independent of the precise details of the bargaining outcome and can be captured in the notions of respect, tolerance and the active cherishing of a variety of ethical stances. These points carry over directly to the imperfectly rational case.

Imperfect rationality, therefore, seems to have its principal impact at the positive rather than the normative level of analysis. With the exception of some additional — but essentially minor — complexity in the ethical bargaining of the pluralist society, there is no real impact on the constitutional and institutional prescriptions discussed in previous sections.

However, two further points of some interest do arise. First, the impact of imperfect rationality at the positive level does carry with it some implications for the nature of legitimate governmental action in an imperfectly rational society. The most obvious case was noticed at the outset of this section, and involves the government in supplying institutions which enforce, as laws, precommitment strategies amongst groups of individuals. Such institutions are explicitly demanded by the relevant individuals, and suffer from no free-rider problem, so this case is relatively straightforward.

A rather more difficult case is raised by the possibility that government may act to supply institutions which have failed to emerge spontaneously, but which would have evolved in a perfectly rational society. This is the case of the government acting as an exogenous improver of individual rationality rather than simply as the provider of mechanisms which allow individuals to adopt their own rationality-improving stratagems.

One apparent difficulty in justifying this type of government action concerns the informational requirements of such a policy. At its starkest the question may be put: how does the government know which institutions to introduce if this is not known by the individuals involved? Furthermore, if the government has additional knowledge why does it need to act rather than simply publish its knowledge and leave action to the individuals? This line of argument is often used against governmental action in the context of the (implicit) assumptions of perfect rationality. But in the imperfectly rational world this argument does not hold.

The first point to note is that, in an imperfectly rational world, different agents have different imperfections so that it is entirely probable that in some (though not all) areas, government does have a more rational and not just better-informed view than some group of potentially involved

individuals. The second point is then that it may be impossible to communicate this more rational view to the imperfectly rational individuals in a way that would elicit the
perfectly rational response. These two points, taken together, indicate that the only means available to government
to act on its more rational view is to act directly to create
the implied institutional reform.

Of course, the government will make mistakes; but such
mistakes can only be recognised ex-post when it can be seen
whether the new institution is self-enforcing and operating
in the predicted manner. If it is not, the experiment can be
aborted.

Government in an imperfectly rational world may legit-
imately engage in the rather speculative development of
novel institutions in an attempt to offset the unpredictable
element in the positive theory of imperfectly rational institutions. Such experimentation will have its failures, and
governmental and constitutional rules may be used to ensure
that such failures are identified and aborted relatively
quickly, whilst the successes cumulate.

The second and final additional point concerning government in an imperfectly rational world refers back to our
notion of effective institutions. It might be recognised that
government will also be populated by imperfectly rational
people.

The implications of this point depend upon the particular
setting. In the neoclassical world in which government was
purely privately motivated, any imperfection renders the
government a less effective monopolist. To the extent that
inefficiency is itself a form of constraint on governmental
power, it can be argued that imperfect rationality acts in
the same way as a constitutional constraint in restraining
the government's ability to pursue its own ends effectively.

In any of the Utopian worlds based on extended rationality, imperfect rationality introduced a degree of heterogeneity into an otherwise homogeneous picture. Because
different individuals will have different imperfections, it
now becomes possible to imagine disagreements on questions of organisation and policy which are not purely empirical in nature. These disagreements will still not be deep in

the sense of arising from fundamentally different ethical positions, but they may be none the less genuine. In this sense, then, imperfect rationality reintroduces politics into Utopia.

In the case of pluralist societies in which the governmental decision-making problem has already been described as insoluble in any computational sense, the introduction of imperfect rationality on the part of the government adds just one further complexity. The possibility of errors due to misperception or other imperfection adds a stochastic element to the political process and renders politics accident prone in the sense that even a well-intended political act, appropriately supported by constitutional rules, may in fact affront the values of some group and so threaten the cohesion of society. Imperfect rationality, in this setting, tests the stability of pluralist society by subjecting it to stochastic political disturbances.

4.6 INDIVIDUALS AND COMMUNITY

The tension between individual rationality and ethics which has formed the theme of this book is often reflected in the debate concerning the relationship between the individual and the community. We have seen that the orthodox economic analysis typically places the individual as the repository of (neoclassical) rationality whilst the government as the embodiment of community is charged with the (Paretian) ethical responsibility.

In slightly broader terms, relationships between the individual and the community depend upon the ethical view taken; a continuum of alternatives exists, but the polar cases reveal the nature of the range.

At one extreme, characterised by deontological libertarianism, is the view that the individual must be supreme over community or any collective, and that rationality must be supreme over any view of the good. In this view, the government must have as its primary (and perhaps only) role the maintenance of an environment of personal inviolability. The community is simply a collection of individuals.

At the opposite extreme, characterised by classical utilitarianism, is the view that the community must be supreme over the individual, and that the ethic must dominate rationality. In this view the government has as its legitimate role the complete structuring of all activities which contribute to the good. The individual is simply the material from which community is built.

However, this range of views of the relationship between the individual and the community operates entirely within the set of Utopias. Each view depends on a particular ethical position held to be the sole relevant criterion. Although the content of each Utopia is distinctive, varying from individualism to communitarianism as suggested by the extremes given above, the form of all Utopias is the same. In the contractarian argument given above, any Utopia must derive from unanimity between individuals each in reflective equilibrium. In this situation each individual actively agrees with the Utopian content, so that even if this is apparently communitarian it is still individualistic in its justification. In this sense the range of views of Utopian relations between the individual and the community obscures the underlying relationship of the consensual community of ethically homogeneous individuals.

The relationship between the individual and the community is of greater interest in the context of pluralist societies. Here each individual has a personal vision of Utopia which conflicts to a greater or lesser extent with the community which he actually inhabits. Furthermore, since different individuals have different visions of Utopia in a pluralist society there is a natural conflict within society. This conflict is a manifestation of the dilemma of commensurability (Section 3.7). It is the existence of incommensurable values within a pluralist society which renders the community-wide decision process of government both problematic and interesting.

Of course, incommensurability is not unique to pluralist societies. Some Utopias will maintain ethical views which incorporate incommensurability; but the situation in pluralist societies differs from these Utopias in two crucial manners. First, the incommensurable values in the pluralist sense are themselves ethical views. We might term this second-order incommensurability. At the first-order level the question of commensurability is the familiar one concerning the possibility of trading off one quantity or value against another. At the second-order level the problem becomes the social one of which of the ethical views available in society should be used in answering the first-order question. Whether incommensurability is held at the first level or not, it must hold at the second level in pluralist societies.

The second distinctive feature of the incommensurability characteristic of pluralistic societies is the absence of any priority rule. In a first-order incommensurable view, such as deontological liberalism, whilst two quantities such as the right and the good are incommensurable at the margin so that no trade-off can be made between them, there is a clear priority rule of the right over the good so that global decision-making can still be undertaken. In the second-order incommensurability of the pluralist society, ethical views are not only incommensurable at the margin but there can be no such priority rule, so decision-making cannot proceed in any criterion-based way.

An implication of this second-order incommensurability of values is that, in pluralist societies, there can be no ultimate appeal to an ethical criterion at the collective or community level. Neither can there be any prospect of producing a community decision function which might act as a surrogate community ethic. No method of compromising, aggregating or otherwise compressing the variety of ethical values present in society can result in a valid social ethic. If the community is to reach decisions these can only came out of the conflict between individually held ethical views by a process of bargaining. This is the prospective contractarian element of the ethical process. As Calabresi and Bobbitt observe:

Morality . . . is not simply the aggregate demands of individuals atomistically wishing to do right. And therefore a moral society must depend upon moral conflict as the basis for determining morality. (Calabresi and Bobbitt, 1978, p. 198)

Some of these points can be illustrated by reference to Table 4.9. In a Paretian Utopia this table would represent the standard tension of circumstance. Both agents would recognise and actively accept the Paretian ethic as the relevant community ethic and so accept institutions, whether emergent or governmental, which resolved the tension.

Equally, in a utilitarian Utopia, each agent would recognise and actively accept the utilitarian ethic which, in the one-shot game, demands an asymmetric outcome in the case of Table 4.9; each individual may therefore be willing to accept an institution which enforces such an outcome even though one agent will certainly be worse off as a result of the institutional reform.

However, if agent 1 is ethically a Paretian whilst agent 2 is a convinced utilitarian, then we have a particularly simple case of a pluralist society. The two agents agree that the equilibrium brought about by direct (ie self-interested) rationality is sub-optimal, so that they both see the benefit of communal action in the form of institutional reform. But they disagree over the appropriate reform precisely because they disagree over the appropriate, communal, ethical criterion.

Imagine the prospective contractarian stage of bargaining between these two agents facing a one-shot version of this pluralists' dilemma and taking the rational equilibrium as the status quo. Agent 1, the Paretian, might notice that his ethically ideal outcome also dominates the rational equilibrium from the point of view of the utilitarian; he might then confidently offer a fully Paretian institution which

Table 4.9: Utopian and Pluralist Dilemmas

		Agent 2	
		A	B
Agent 1	A	(10,10)	(0,30)
	B	(30,0)	(1,1)

enforces strategy A for both agents. In response to this, agent 2, the utilitarian, might counter-offer an institution which binds himself to strategy A whilst allowing agent 1 to choose strategy B and so free-ride.

How would the agents choose between these alternative institutions? Agent 1, by assumption, prefers his own proposal on ethical grounds, but the counter-offer is very tempting since it dominates the alternative on the criterion of self-interest. For agent 2 the situation is reversed; his counter-offer is ethically superior but involves a considerable sacrifice in self-interested terms. In this situation there is clear conflict between narrow self-interested rationality and ethics, but this tension is internal to each individual and not representative of a relationship between the individual and a broader community which carries some ethical force. Indeed, the internal tension arises because, at the social level, there is no well-defined ethical force. Given this internal tension we cannot predict the final outcome of this prospective contractarian bargain without knowing the relative strengths of the two individuals' commitments to self-interest and to their particular ethical view, within the overall framework of their extended rationality.

This simple example of pluralist society stresses that the site of the tension between self-interest and ethics lies within the individual and within the notion of extended rationality, rather than between the individual and the abstract community.

In this view, the community is a forum in which individuals operate, held together by mutually agreed rules which are borne not out of consensus on ethical matters but out of the need to ensure tolerance and respect if individuals are to live together and share in the gains of collective action. These constitutional rules reflect the variety of ethical positions rather than the dominance of any particular Utopian view.

Government in such a community is not conceived as an ethical force in itself; rather it is an agency designed — perhaps poorly — to respond to the needs of the ethical views of the members of the community, whatever these might be. In our example the government might be called upon to enforce either a utilitarian or a Paretian institution. In a slightly broader example it would be easy to imagine a government providing Paretian and utilitarian institutions and policies simultaneously. Ethical consistency in government policy may be of no particular value in a pluralist society and, at the limit, may be of negative value if those who hold alternative views lose respect for the community which acts as if it has no respect for their views.

4.7 POLITICS

Politics encompasses the process of social decision-making which provides for influential linkages running between individuals, the constitution, and government; and so on to the policies and actions of government which ultimately operate on individuals. For our present purposes, politics can be viewed as consisting of three basic elements, one concerning the linkages between individuals and government, a second concerning the linkages involving the constitution with either individuals or government, and a third concerned with the process of decision-making within government.

The discussion of the previous sections has already raised a number of points on the nature of politics in each of the fully neoclassical society, the Utopian society and the pluralist society. These points can now be drawn together.

In the fully neoclassical society both the linkages between individuals and government, and the decision-making process within government, degenerate into the pursuit of self-interest. The political communication between individuals and government consists simply of individuals engaging in special pleading either singly or in pressure groups. Special pleas, in this view, must always be seen as self-interested and individuals will search for government preferment just as long as the expected benefits outweigh the costs. The same rational cost–benefit analysis will typify the individual's decision to vote or otherwise participate in the political process. Only if the participation offers direct and personal benefits in excess of the costs will the individual proceed.

Within government, individual politicians will adopt policy positions purely with an eye to their own long-term self-interest. In particular cases this may lie in re-election, or in gaining favour within a political party, or in ensuring post-political employment by gaining potential advantages for potential employers; but whatever form it takes, actual policies emerge as the result of bargaining between self-interested politicians which can be expected to involve log-rolling and other gambits.

The political process in the neoclassical world is distinguished from other parts of society not by any difference in the motivations of the agents involved, but rather by the nature of the constraints imposed on those actors. It is in this third aspect of politics, the linkages involving the constitution, that we find the distinctly political component which attempts to lift the practice of politics above the simple pursuit of self-interest. The constitution aims to limit governmental discretion and so channel governmental actions along ethically desirable lines — or at least away from ethically undesirable lines. However, we have argued that the narrow conception of individual rationality makes it difficult to ground any particular ethic and so the ethical force embodied in the neoclassical constitution can be, at best, only weak.

That there might be any contractarian agreement on a limiting constitution which establishes and justifies government, places government on a rank above the range of emergent institutions which arise spontaneously out of a direct consideration of individual rationality. But the weakness of the contractarian method stripped of any individually relevant Archimedean point, and the consequent weakness of the constitution, strips politics of much of its potential force.

In a Utopian setting — whichever particular Utopia is involved — the political linkages are entirely different, although the constitution is again the central political feature. The Utopian constitution embodies the strong ethical view of all individuals and so establishes a unique and well-defined criterion which is to be used in making all social and governmental choices. Such a constitution replaces governmental discretion so that decision-making within government becomes entirely automatic and computational in nature. At the same time, the nature and clarity of the constitution ensures that there is no requirement for in-period political communication between individuals and government. The constitution already contains the population's final and unanimous word on government, and each individual, in actively agreeing to the constitution, precommits his obligation to the constitutional, and hence ethical, government.

I have already suggested that Utopias are natural one-party states; but even this understates the effective depoliticisation of government in Utopia. It would be more appropriate to think of government as an entirely technical exercise entrusted to specifically trained civil servants, rather than a political exercise calling for judgement, responsibility, representation and so on.

It might be said that whilst neoclassical society is beneath politics, since it lacks any broader social commitment, Utopian societies are above politics since they lack the diversity of view essential to a political debate.

In the pluralist society, politics is of the essence. All three elements of the political process are of major importance, with no one of them dominating the others. The constitution in a pluralist society lacks the ethical unity of a Utopian constitution and so cannot fully precommit government. Nevertheless, since the constitution can be seen as the outcome of a prospective contractarian bargain between ethically informed individuals, it does carry a considerable force in restraining government. We have already suggested that respect for alternative ethical views, individual tolerance, the frequent reform of political institution, and the vulnerability of government will all be incorporated into pluralist constitution.

Individuals in a pluralist society are the source of the variety of ethical views and can be expected to participate in the political process in support of their own particular commitments, which include, but are not restricted to, their own self-interest.

The political problem in pluralist society is markedly different from that found in either neoclassical or Utopian societies. In each of these cases government and individual politicians had the benefit of clear guidance as to their behaviour and decision-making. In the pluralist case the problem is precisely the making of decisions in the absence of any such clear guidance. The presence of second order incommensurability implied by the individualistic variety of ethical views ensures that political problems are insoluble. Government is then the body which is delegated the task of making impossible decisions.

Government, in this setting, takes on a very particular role. It is not appropriate to picture government as an independent ethical force, nor is it appropriate to view government as the leader of society; rather, government is the particular forum chosen to cope with the set of issues which are potentially socially divisive since they bring ethical views into conflict. Politics and government are, therefore, a sort of neutral zone in which these issues can be debated and decided within the procedural rules agreed and laid down in the constitution, without the individuals who "lose" on any particular issue taking offence at society. In this view, an important feature of the political process in a pluralist society which is totally absent in either the neoclassical society or any Utopia, is not that it chooses the right option, but that it allows the losers to lose with honour and retain their values within society whilst accepting a degree of obligation to the governmental decision.

In relating this discussion to the tension between individual rationality and ethics we may note that in the fully neoclassical world the ethic is embodied only in the constitution so that the tension is played out in the operation of government against its constraints. In this world politics has little or no ethical content and is simply rational bargaining writ large.

In Utopia, the ethic is sufficiently clearly defined to extend its domain from the constitution to government, so that the picture of government as an essentially ethical agent which is characteristic of the naive economic view is reinstated in Utopia. The tension between individual rationality and ethics is then formally located at the interface between individuals and government; but since government has legitimate authority over individuals in Utopia, the tension disappears. In this world politics has no problem to solve.

In the pluralist society the tension operates at two levels, first within the individual, and second between individuals who hold distinct ethical views. Both the constitution and the government are then seen as devices — ethically neutral in themselves — which are designed to assist in the resolution of these tensions and their accompanying impossible decisions. In this world the political process itself embodies the tension between rationality and ethics.

4.8   INTERIM CONCLUSIONS

This chapter has utilised the generalised contractarian method to investigate the fundamental implications of alternative theories of rationality for the institutional and constitional structure of society, and the nature of the relationships between individuals and the state. Two aspects of this discussion have been stressed. First, the variety of roles played by a theory of rationality in any evaluation of social institutions has been emphasised. This discussion provided us with the notion of an "effective institution" as one which is designed in recognition of the full range of implications of rational behaviour. Such an institution may be described as being rationally designed to be operated by rational individuals with the purpose of influencing rational behaviour in the direction of an ethical criterion which is itself grounded in rationality.

The second aspect of the discussion which has been emphasised is the distinction between those institutions which can be expected to emerge directly out of a particular notion of rationality, and the question of the ethical justification of those institutions. This distinction is clearly contrary to the spirit of the invisible hand theory of the state presented by Nozick.

In making his major argument for the liberal or libertarian state (Section 3.4), Nozick makes considerable use of the entitlement principle.[25] This principle claims that an outcome is justified if it arises from an earlier justified position by means of justified procedures:

As correct rules of inference are truth-preserving, and any conclusion deduced via repeated application of such rules from only true premisses is itself true, so the means of transition from one situation to another specified by the principle of justice in transfer are justice-preserving, and any situation actually arising from repeated transitions in accordance with the principle from a just situation is itself just. (Nozick, 1974, p. 151)

This principle underlies the justification of the Nozickian state which is argued to emerge from the (assumed justified) Lockean state of nature by processes which infringe no individual rights.

However, it is doubtful that the entitlement principle is valid — at least for repeated applications of the procedure.[26] In place of the analogy with the correct rules of inference, consider the following: if you are healthy and engage in a health-preserving activity (or even a health-promoting activity) then you will be healthy. This statement has the same form as the entitlement principle and is similarly true for single applications, but there can be no presumption of validity in the case of repeated applications. There are many actions which are health-preserving (or health-promoting) when done once, but which are fatal if repeated frequently.

Threshold effects of this kind may characterise the operation of society in the Nozickian process of state formation. For example, the private accumulation of property in small amounts may be fully consistent with the liberty and rights of others, but such accumulation carried beyond a certain point (which may be well short of full monopolisation) may begin to encroach upon the liberty of others as monopoly power is created.[27]

Both because the general validity of the entitlement principle is doubtful, and because of the difficulty in establishing, *a priori*, the Archimedean nature of the operation of individual rationality, it is impossible to conclude that whatever institutions emerge from rational behaviour are justified. The further work that needs to be done has occupied a considerable part of this chapter.

In sketching out the basic implications of alternative theories of rationality for the emergence of social institutions, we have focussed on the possibility of the emergence of institutions as external aids to individual strategies of (binding or non-binding) precommitment which may derive from either imperfect or extended views of rationality. Such institutions and laws differ markedly from those associated with the neoclassical approach to rationality, which views institutions as essentially inter-personal rather than intra-personal devices.

The parallel discussion of the justification of institutions has taken the constitution and its impact on government as the major point of interest, and utilised the contractarian method to provide a categorisation of the types of constitutional outcomes associated with each view of rationality. Of primary importance here was the distinction between Utopia and pluralism, where each of these terms carries a meaning specific to this context: Utopia being any society in which there is unanimous agreement on the ethical criterion of relevance, whilst pluralist societies form the complementary set of societies in which there is unresolved, and unresolvable, ethical debate.

The distinction between the purely neoclassically rational society, the set of Utopias, and the set of pluralist societies, provided the basis for a discussion of the alternative possible relationships between the individual and the society in which he lives, and a characterisation of politics which suggests that truly political processes are associated only with pluralist societies which lack any ultimate criterion for social action.

5 Epilogue

The explorations contained in this book have ranged fairly widely and have often followed indirect routes. It is therefore appropriate to end by attempting to restate the major line of argument developed throughout the book. The bald statement of this main line of argument will inevitably ignore many of the points of interest which have been encountered along the way, and it will not even attempt to summarise the arguments put. It simply serves to remind us of the overall pattern of the journey so as to place the various points of interest and specific arguments in the wider context.

Our starting point has been the orthodox neoclassical economic viewpoint with its particular views of rationality and ethics. This viewpoint provides a theory of institutions and their justification which may be crudely summarised as follows. Individual rationality, working from the bottom up, results in the emergence of a range of institutions. At the same time government, acting as an ethical agent from the top down, controls these emergent institutions and supplements them in the public interest.

This neoclassical view is well illustrated in the standard prisoners' dilemma, made up of the exogenously imposed definitions of rationality and the Pareto criterion, which are then used to support the claim that if an institutional device to ensure cooperation does not evolve spontaneously, government should enforce this solution as an ethically desirable improvement over the sub-optimal rational equilibrium.

We have questioned this argument at each stage. The relevant concept of rationality has been examined in some detail, and alternatives suggested. These alternatives provide a more detailed internal structure to the individual decision-maker and are characterised principally by their admission of a moral dimension and by the existence of internal tensions which may be partially relieved by acts of self-commitment or precommitment.

Alternative substantive ethical theories have been examined in some detail and, most importantly, the contractarian ethical method has been argued to provide a link between particular concepts of individual rationality and particular substantive ethics. The distinction between hypothetical and prospective contractarian has been developed, and the authority of each has been argued to depend upon the recognition of an Archimedean point. One essential feature of such an Archimedean point is a concept of rationality. The Rawlsian concept of reflective equilibrium has been utilised in focussing particular attention on a sub-class of contractarian bargaining outcomes, but the wide variety of positions derivable from the contractarian method has been emphasised.

The position of government as an ethical agent has been questioned and replaced by a view of government as an effective institution which operates via the rational actions of its members within a framework of rules provided by a constitution. This constitution derives from the contractarian method and is, therefore, based on an explicitly recognised view of rationality. The contractarian constitutional view therefore endogenises the role of government and the ethical content of a constitution within the institutional debate.

Given alternative concepts of rationality, the contractarian method, and the constitutional framework of effective government, we have identified three distinct types of society. Within each type we have then enquired as to the general nature of the emergent institutions and the role of constitutional government in restraining and supplementing these institutions. Each type of society emphasises a different aspect of the potential tension between individual rationality and ethics, and a different social approach to the resolution of this tension.

At one extreme we have the narrowly neoclassical society in which self-interest is the only motivation of individual action. At the opposite extreme we have the set of Utopias, each upholding a particular substantive ethical view to the exclusion of all ethical debate. Between these extremes we have pluralist societies in which many ethical views exist simultaneously with no one of them dominating and no possibility of the identification of any single social ethic.

In the narrowly neoclassical world, government is not an ethical agent and there can be no guarantee that emergent institutions will be controlled or supplemented in the light of any particular ethical view. A constitution may derive from the contractarian process which establishes and justifies a form of government, but this process can be seen as simply an extension of rational bargaining which carries little or no ethical backing or justificatory force. At the limit, government is just another emergent institution.

In the sense, this illustrates the proposition that, in the fully neoclassical world, the ethical criterion is redundant or, more accurately, subsumed within the notion of rationality. Within any particular institutional framework perfect neoclassical rationality ensures the elimination of all potential gains from exchange and so ensures what might be termed a "local" Pareto optimality. Similarly, at the constitutional level, institutions will emerge if and only if they make accessible greater gains from exchange. Such institutions ensure "global" Pareto optimality.

This Panglossian world in which rationality at every level entails Pareto efficiency, eliminates all tension between rationality and ethics by placing total weight on rationality. It is in this sense — and only this sense — that neoclassical economists may claim that the Pareto criterion is a minimalist ethic once perfect neoclassical rationality has been assumed (Section 3.3).

In a Utopian world, government has, by the contractarian route, ethical authority which is fully precommitted by a strong constitution, but government also commands complete and legitimate authority over individuals within its constitutional limits. In such a world there is again no real tension between individual rationality and the well-defined social ethic; each has its realm of dominance and there are no grey areas of tension or dispute. Government is an automatic procedure in Utopia, and politics has no role to play.

In a pluralist world the interpretations of the constitution and government change dramatically. There is no longer any specific ethical authority embodied in either of these institutions and attention focusses instead on the tensions between alternative ethical views held by different individuals. The contractarian argument distinguishes between the hypothetical contractarian exercise within each individual, and the prospective contractarian exercise between individuals. Government, in this view, is argued not to operate from the top down in leading society from a particular ethical position, but rather to operate as a forum which operationalises the prospective contractarian exercise in such a way as to ensure social cohesion. The constitution in such a society is primarily concerned with structuring this forum to ensure that the government process respects alternative ethical views so that it can hope to gain the respect and obligation of individuals.

In the course of this book we have moved from the very special case of the prisoners' dilemma incorporating a narrow view of rationality and an exogenously imposed view of ethics to a much more general view of the same problem. Our more general view allows for an extended and imperfect rationality and also allows each individual his own, endogenously determined ethical view. This pluralists' dilemma then exemplifies the prospective contractarian stage of the pluralist society where institutions can emerge from ethical bargaining in the context of the governmental process just as, in the narrowly economic model, they emerge from rational bargaining between individuals.

Pluralist society faces impossible problems which arise out of the incommensurability of alternative ethical views. The hallmark of constitutional government in such a society is the ability to cope with such problems without being socially divisive.

The form of tension between individual self-interest and ethics with which we began this book is very different from the form of tension with which we end it. In each case the tension can justify an institutional resolution, but the site of the tension, its grounding and the process of institutional reform called for is very different as between the two views.

Of course, the arguments put in this book have not been sufficient to do more than outline a systematic approach to the complex and interrelated set of issues; nor has the discussion drawn out the full implications of the views and arguments outlined. If the presentation has stimulated interest in developing or criticising these views and arguments it has achieved its purpose.

Notes

CHAPTER 1

1. For classic discussion *see* Luce and Raiffa (1957), Schelling (1960), Shubik (1982). For discussion of the prisoners' dilemma in contexts related to the present discussion *see* Runciman and Sen (1965), Gauthier (1967), Ullmann-Margalit (1977), Schelling (1978), Parfit (1979), Schotter (1981), Barry and Hardin (1982).
2. Strictly, the requirement is for either an infinite number of repetitions or for an uncertain number so that the final round of the game is never identifiable ex-ante; *see* Luce and Raiffa (1967). Alternatively, one or both of the agents may be unsure of their opponent's rationality, or both agents may be unsure of the precise pay-offs. A number of alternative specifications of uncertainty will allow cooperation as part of an equilibrium strategy; *see* Kreps, Milgrom, Roberts and Wilson (1982). For empirical studies of the repeated prisoners' dilemma *see* Axelrod (1981, 1984) and references therein.
3. One possibility is that the state uses its authority to ensure repetition of the game, so encouraging a cooperative solution. The point here is that this is an example of the third approach and not the second, since the state is operating with externally generated authority to transform the "natural" game into a repeated game.
4. This modified prisoners' dilemma differs from the standard formulation in the specification of the ethical criterion and in that in the ethically desirable position only one of the agents faces a private incentive to change strategy.
5. For a recent welfare economics text which provides some explicit discussion of alternative ethical rules, *see* Boadway and Bruce (1984).

CHAPTER 2

1. The interested reader is recommended to read Anscombe (1957), Norman (1971), Benn and Mortimore (1976), Baier (1977), Gibson (1977), Harrison (1979) and Taylor, C. (1982) in addition to the more specific references contained in this chapter.
2. For an influential statement of the relativist position *see* Winch (1964); for discussion *see* Wilson (1970) and Hollis and Lukes (1982).
3. Note that this does not imply that all actions are subjectively belief-rational. It is clearly possible to imagine individuals acting in conflict with their own underlying belief-model, eg "instinctively" braking when your car skids even though you "know" this to be inappropriate. However, the rain-dancing tribesman of the earlier example would be subjectively belief-rational if he is sincere.
4. "Formal" and "substantive" are used here in the sense of Parfit (1984), ie "According to all moral theories, we ought to try to act morally. According to all theories about rationality, we ought to try to act rationally. Call these our *formal* aims. Different moral theories, and different theories about rationality, give us different *substantive* aims." (Parfit, 1984, p. 3. Emphasis in original).
5. *See* for example Collard (1975), Sen (1977) and Hollis (1979). Collard and Sen rightly point out that, despite the "only" in the quoted passage, Edgeworth did not view egoism as the only motivation covering all human action; rather his view was that self-interest was the fundamental motivation in specifically economic action.
6. On the distinction between local and global maximisation as the basis of rationality *see* Elster (1984) pp. 4–18.
7. Characteristics (i), (v) and (vi) are identified in Sen (1977), pp. 342–3.
8. For critical comment on perfect information seen as an assumption additional to any notion of rationality *see* Hollis and Nell (1975).
9. *See* Simon (1954, 1976, 1978a, 1978b, 1983).
10. This problem area is also referred to as the problem of incontinence or akrasia; *see* Schelling (1980, 1983) and Elster (1984).
11. Of considerable influence in philosophy and economics respectively are Sidgwick (1907) and Ramsey (1928).
12. *See also* pp. 293–8.

13. Elster (1984) pp. 67–8.
14. Parfit (1984) pp. 117–94.
15. For more detailed discussion of the problems of endogenously changing preferences and time preferences *see* Strotz (1955), Weizsacker (1971), Parfit (1973), Hollis and Nell (1975) and Elster (1982, 1983, 1984).
16. For discussion of this infinite regress *see* Winter (1964) and Elster (1984).
17. This conclusion does not imply that it cannot be rational to *behave* irrationally. However, this is not in itself evidence of bounded rationality, see Parfit (1984) Section 5.
18. Simon (1954, 1976).
19. For detailed discussion and many examples *see* Schelling (1980, 1983) and Elster (1984).
20. Weakness of will is, however, neither necessary nor sufficient for inconsistency.
21. For a discussion of altruism in the early economics literature *see* Collard (1978) Chapter 6; the remainder of that book outlines the modern debate. *See also* Nagel (1970), Phelps (1975), Sugden (1982) and Elster (1984).
22. This argument is put more fully, and the empirical predictions spelled out more clearly, in Sugden (1982).
23. Margolis (1982) Chapter 3 provides an example. For further criticism *see* Elster (1984) pp. 141–6.
24. For detailed discussion of the concept of an evolutionary-stable strategy *see* Maynard-Smith (1973).
25. The required condition is that:

$$0(1-w) + 12(w) > 5(1-w) + 5w$$

ie $w > \dfrac{5}{12}$.

26. An assurance game is defined as one in which the outcomes are ranked by agent 1 in the following order (with agent 1's strategy listed first): Cooperate–Cooperate/Compete–Cooperate/Compete–Compete/Cooperate–Compete. The condition for this in the context of Table 2.3 is that:

$$10(1-w) + 10(w) > 12(1-w) + 0 > 5(1-w) + 5(w) > 0 + 12w$$

ie $\dfrac{2}{12} < w < \dfrac{5}{12}$.

For detailed discussion of assurance games *see* Sen (1967, 1973).
27. The condition is that the expected pay-off from cooperating must exceed the expected pay-off from competing, so that:

$$10(1-w)p + 10wp + 0 + 12w(1-p) > 12(1-w)p + 0 + 5(1-w)(1-p) + 5w(1-p)$$

ie $p > \dfrac{5}{3} - 4w$.

28. *See* Sen (1977) and Broome (1978b).
29. Collard (1978), Margolis (1982) pp. 36–46, Sugden (1984) pp. 773–5.
30. Sen (1977) p. 326.
31. The most frequently quoted empirical critique is Kahneman and Tversky (1979). For a review of the related literature *see* Schoemaker (1982).
32. More detailed and precise statements can be found in Schoemaker (1982), Machina (1982), Luce and Riaffa (1957) and Marschak (1950).
33. Kahneman and Tversky (1979) p. 256.
34. *Ibid.* pp. 256–7.
35. *Ibid.* pp. 271–2.
36. ie, That the preference function is differentiable with respect to the probabilities; *see* Machina (1982) pp. 293–5.
37. *Ibid.* pp. 302–6.
38. *See* Schoemaker (1982) p. 555 and references therein.
39. Loomes and Sugden (1982) pp. 815–16.
40. For extended discussion of the subjectivist critique and a more positive account of a subjectivist account of action *see* Shackle (1972) and Loasby (1976).
41. On the distinctions between institutional and moral rights *see* Macpherson (1978), Lyons (1980), Brandt (1983).
42. In terms of the discussion of alternative approaches to the avoidance of the standard prisoners' dilemma (*see* Chapter 1), a norm arises out of the second approach whilst a law corresponds to the third approach.
43. Hohfeld (1923).

CHAPTER 3

1. For a more general discussion *see*, for example, Brandt (1959), Williams (1972) and Mackie (1977).

2. As portrayed in Sidgwick (1907). *See* Lyons (1965) for discussion of a variety of forms of utilitarianism.
3. Sen (1979b).
4. Lyons (1965), Smart and Williams (1973).
5. For versions of this argument *see* Harsanyi (1953) and Hare (1976).
6. For detailed discussion *see* Harsanyi (1955), Mirrlees (1982) and Broome (1983).
7. In addition to the 1955 paper *see* Harsanyi (1975b, 1977, 1978).
8. Broome (1983) p. 19.
9. Broome (1983) pp. 46–8.
10. The argument against commensurability is put in Williams (1972). *See* the discussion in Griffin (1977).
11. Harsanyi (1955) provides details.
12. Note the strong resemblance between this example and that in Table 3.1; both hinge on the valuation of distribution and uncertainty.
13. *See*, for example, Broome (1978a, 1984), Hammond (1981, 1982), Ulph (1982). Hamlin (1984b) presents some further discussion.
14. For a critical discussion *see* Nath (1969). A careful exposition of the basic welfare theory and its dependence on Paretian values can be found in Boadway and Bruce (1984).
15. Boadway and Bruce (1984) pp. 96–102.
16. *See* Hamlin (1983) and references therein, particularly Buchanan (1975b, 1977).
17. *See* the discussion of Buchanan's position in Barry, N. (1984).
18. For example, Sen (1970, 1976), Rawls (1971), Hayek (1973, 1976, 1979), Nozick (1974), Rowley and Peacock (1975) and Sandel (1982).
19. For a historical review *see* Girvetz (1963); for a more discursive view *see* Minogue (1963). Sandel (1984) reviews a number of contemporary positions.
20. For example, *see* Hayek (1960), p. 19 and Berlin (1969).,
21. Rowley and Peacock (1975) pp. 85–90.
22. For a discussion of the conflict between freedom as means and as an end in Hayek, *see* Hamlin (1983).
23. *See* the discussion of Mill's "Romantic libertarianism" in Gibbs (1976).
24. For a fuller discussion of this division *see* Sandel (1982).
25. Each of these books has spawned a large literature. *See*, for example, Buchanan (1972, 1975a), Barry, B. (1973, 1980), Daniels (1974), Harsanyi (1975a), Gordon (1976), Clark and Gintis (1978), Chapman (1983) and Barry, N. (1984).

26. Nozick (1974) pp. 174–82.
27. *Ibid.* pp. 30–5.
28. Buchanan (1975b, 1977), Buchanan and Tullock (1962).
29. This is in contrast to Nozick where only a protective state is argued to be justified. For critical discussion of Buchanan's argument *see* Barry, B. (1980) and Barry, N. (1984).
30. By Buchanan (1975a) amongst others.
31. Rawls (1971) Sections 39 and 82.
32. For a contrast between liberal individualism and free market individualism *see* Hamlin (1983).
33. On this point *see* the distinction between the market and the meta-market in Buchanan's views in Hamlin (1984b).
34. The debate following this article is surveyed and commented upon in Sen (1976). (*See* references therein and also Chapman (1983) and Mueller (1979) pp. 201–6.)
35. Rawls (1971) p. 16. *See* Hamlin (1984b) for a distinction between "naive", "hypothetical" and "prospective" contractarianism. For a related discussion of contractarianism *see* Scanlon (1982).
36. Rawls (1971) pp. 17–21, 577–87.
37. *Ibid.* pp. 48–51; for commentary *see* Barry, B. (1973) Chapter 2 and Sandel (1982) pp. 40–6.
38. Rawls (1971) pp. 121–2.
39. For example, Honderich (1976), Dworkin (1977).
40. Buchanan (1975a).
41. Hamlin (1984a) discusses the forms of constitutional control available to such individuals.
42. Technically, the core is defined in terms of the minimum payoffs (or withdrawal rule) of each possible coalition of agents, in addition to those of each individual agent. In the example it is natural to assume that each coalition is the simple sum of its members, and nothing of significance will depend on this aspect of the definition of the core. For a more detailed discussion *see* Arrow and Hahn (1971).
43. *See* Rawls (1971) pp. 60–7 for a full statement.
44. It is the need to *guarantee* an improvement which introduces extreme risk aversion into the Rawlsian bargain; *see* Howe and Roemer (1981) pp. 882–3.
45. *Ibid.* pp. 883–4.
46. Rawls (1971) p. 179.
47. Nozick (1974) pp. 228–31.
48. Sandel (1982) pp. 77–82.
49. Rawls (1971) p. 27.

50. In a world where labour was the only factor this is the standard problem of returns to scale. But if other factors exist there will be a surplus over the marginal products of labour even if society is a constant returns to scale activity.
51. *See* Buchanan and Faith (1980)
52. Rawls (1971) p. 86.
53. For more general discussions of Marxian exploitation in the context of his political economy *see* Bose (1980) and Morishima (1974).
54. Coercion and exploitation are linked, but the precise nature of the link is contentious. Most would agree that coercion implies exploitation, but whether coercion is a necessary condition for exploitation is doubtful; *see* Wood (1979) pp. 279–80, and the discussion of Nozick's view of exploitation below.
55. But *see* Husami (1978).
56. This point is very similar to Rawls' view of the ethical arbitrariness of a person's endowments; *see* Section 3.5.
57. Brenkert (1979), Cohen (1979), Roemer (1982a); but *see* Wolff (1981).
58. Roemer (1982b, 1982c, 1982d).
59. Compare Howe and Roemer (1981) with Roemer (1982d).
60. Roemer (1982c, 1982d).
61. Sen (1982) pp. 7–12.
62. Nozick (1974) pp. 28–33.
63. *Ibid*. p. 166.
64. *Ibid*. p. 28.
65. Griffin (1977) p. 49; *see also* pp. 55–6.
66. Nozick (1974), p. 331.
67. *See*, for example, Peffer (1978).
68. Rawls (1971) pp. 13–14. But *see* the discussion of Sandel's interpretation of Rawls in Section 3.5 above.
69. *See* Section 3.5 above.
70. For the Rawlsian schema recast in Buchanan's terms *see* Buchanan and Faith (1980).
71. *See* Rawls (1971) pp. 34–40, Barry, B. (1965) and Gordon (1980).
72. *See*, for example, Parfit (1984) pp. 391–3.

CHAPTER 4

1. The classic references are Coase (1937) and Williamson (1975).

2. Buchanan (1965).
3. Baumol (1952) provides an excellent discussion of this view in the context of the early writers in political economy. Whynes and Bowles (1981) also take this as the starting point.
4. *See* particularly Schelling (1960), Ullmann–Margalit (1977) and Schotter (1981).
5. Schelling (1960) pp. 83–9.
6. Ullmann-Margalit (1977) Chapter 4. Such norms are termed "inequality preserving institutions" by Schotter (1981).
7. Axelrod (1981, 1984).
8. Effectively, the law is providing each agent with an assurance that the other agent will adopt strategy A. *See* the discussion of assurance games in Section 5. Note that Table 4.8(b) is essentially identical to Table 4.1.
9. For a classic discussion of this problem *see* Olson (1965).
10. Particularly important contributions were made by Downs (1957) and Black (1958). For a survey *see* Mueller (1979).
11. Constitutional constraints of a procedural nature are stressed in Buchanan and Tullock (1962); constraints which directly limit governmental actions are discussed in Brennan and Buchanan (1980).
12. This argument is put in detail in Hamlin (1984a).
13. Sen (1977).
14. This definition extends that presented in Nozick (1974) Chapter 10. As we have already seen (Sections 3.4, 3.5), the Nozickian Utopia derives from a particular specification of the withdrawal rule relevant at the hypothetical contractarian stage of the ethical process. Nozick effectively argues for a procedural view of Utopia at the second stage whilst apparently inserting a particular and arbitrary starting point for the first stage.
15. *See*, for example, Buchanan and Tullock (1962), Wolff (1970).
16. Taylor, M. (1982) pp. 25–33.
17. Olson (1965).
18. Taylor's three properties of community are clearly necessary conditions for anarchy and not sufficient conditions.
19. *See* Gordon (1980) pp. 41–9 for a similar, though not identical, account of pluralism.
20. For further discussion of alternative forms of individualism *see* Hamlin (1983).
21. Recall Taylor, M. (1982) and the properties of "community".
22. Calabresi and Bobbitt (1978).
23. This point is discussed more fully in Section 4.6 below.

24. *See* Section 4.2, particular Tables 4.3 and 4.4 and the associated text.
25. For a full statement *see* Nozick (1974) pp. 150–3.
26. This discussion is based on Reiman (1981).
27. Compare Reiman (1981) pp. 89–93 with Nozick (1974) pp. 178–82.

References

Anscombe, G. E. M. (1957) *Intention*, Cornell University Press.

Arrow, K. and Hahn, F. (1971) *General Competitive Analysis*, Oliver and Boyd.

Axelrod, R. (1981) "The emergence of cooperation among egoists", *American Political Science Review*, Vol. 75, pp. 306–18.

——(1984) *The Evolution of Cooperation*, Basic Books.

Baier, K. (1977) "Rationality and morality", *Erkenntnis*, vol. 11, pp. 197–223.

Barry, B. (1965) *Political Argument*, Routledge and Kegan Paul.

——(1973) *The Liberal Theory of Justice*, Oxford University Press.

——(1980) Review in *Theory and Decision*, Vol. 12, pp. 95–106.

Barry, B. and Hardin, R. (eds.) (1982) *Rational Man and Irrational Society?* Sage.

Barry, N. (1984) "Unanimity, agreement and liberalism — a critique of James Buchanan's social philosophy", *Political Theory*, Vol. 12, pp. 579–96.

Baumol, W. J. (1952) *Welfare Economics and the Theory of the State*, Longman.

Benn, S. I., and Mortimore, G. W. (eds) (1976) *Rationality and the Social Sciences*, Routledge and Kegan Paul.

Berlin, I. (1969) *Four Essays on Liberty*, Oxford University Press.

Black, D. (1958) *The Theory of Committees and Elections*, Cambridge University Press.

Boadway, R. and Bruce, N. (1984) *Welfare Economics*, Basil Blackwell.

Bose, A. (1980) *Marx on Exploitation and Inequality: An Essay in Marxian and Analytical Economics*, Oxford University Press.

Brandt, R. B. (1959) *Ethical Theory*, Prentice Hall.

——(1983) "The concept of a moral right and its function", *Journal of Philosophy*, Vol. 80, pp. 29–45.

Brenkert, G. G. (1979) "Freedom and private property in Marx",

Philosophy and Public Affairs, Vol. 8, pp. 122–47.

Brennan, G. and Buchanan, J. M. (1980) *The Power to Tax*, Cambridge University Press.

Breton, A. (1974) *The Economic Theory of Representative Government*, Aldine-Atherton, Chicago.

Broome, J. (1978a) "Trying to value a life", *Journal of Public Economics*, Vol. 9, pp. 91–100.

——(1978b) "Rational choice and value in economics", *Oxford Economic Papers*, Vol. 30, pp. 313–33.

——(1983) "Utilitarianism and separability", *Discussion Paper*, University of Bristol.

——(1984) "Uncertainty and fairness", *Economic Journal*, Vol. 94, pp. 624–32.

Buchanan, J. M. (1964) "What should economists do? " *Southern Economic Journal*, Vol. 30, pp. 213–22.

——(1965) "An economic theory of clubs", *Economica*, Vol. 32, pp. 1–14.

——(1972) "Rawls on justice and fairness", *Public Choice*, Vol. 13, pp. 123–8.

——(1975a) "Utopia, the minimal state, and entitlement", *Public Choice*, Vol. 22, pp. 121–6.

——(1975b) *The limits of Liberty: Between Anarchy and Leviathan*, University of Chicago Press.

——(1977) *Freedom in Constitutional Contract*, Texas A & M University Press.

Buchanan, J. M. and Faith, R. L. (1980) "Subjective elements in Rawlsian contractual agreement on distributional rules", *Economic Inquiry*, Vol. 18, pp. 23–38.

Buchanan, J. M. and Tullock, G. (1962) *The Calculus of Consent*, University of Michigan Press.

Calabresi, G. and Bobbitt, P. (1978) *Tragic Choices*, Norton.

Chapman, B. (1983) "Rights as constraints: Nozick versus Sen", *Theory and Decision*, Vol. 15, pp. 1–10.

Clark, B. and Gintis, H. (1978) "Rawlsian justice and economic systems", *Philosophy and Public Affairs*, Vol. 7, pp. 302–25.

Coase, R. (1937) "The nature of the firm", *Economica*, Vol. 4, pp. 386–405.

Cohen, G. A. (1979) "The labour theory of value and the concept of exploitation", *Philosophy and Public Affairs*, Vol. 8, pp. 338–60.

Collard, D. (1975) "Edgeworth's propositions on altruism", *Economic Journal*, Vol. 85, pp. 335–60.

——(1978) *Altruism and Economy,* Martin Robertson.

Daniels, N. (ed.) (1974) *Reading Rawls*, Basic Books.

188 *Ethics, Economics and the State*

Diamond, P. A. (1967) "Cardinal welfare, individualistic ethics, and interpersonal comparisons of utility: comment", *Journal of Political Economy*, Vol. 75, pp. 765–6.

Downs, A. (1957) *An Economic Theory of Democracy*, Harper and Row.

Dworkin, R. (1977) *Taking Rights Seriously*, Duckworth.

Edgeworth, F. Y. (1881) *Mathematical Psychics*, Routledge and Kegan Paul.

Elster, J. (1982) "Sour grapes — utilitarianism and the genesis of wants", in Sen, A. K. and Williams, B. A. O. (eds.) (1982) *Utilitarianism and Beyond*, Cambridge University Press.

——(1983) *Sour Grapes*, Cambridge University Press.

——(1984) *Ulysses and the Sirens*, (rev. edn.), Cambridge University Press.

Feinberg, J. (1970) "The nature and value of rights", *Journal of Value Inquiry*, Vol. 4, pp. 243–57.

Gauthier, D. P. (1967) "Morality and Advantage", *Philosophical Review*, Vol. 76, pp. 460–75.

Gibbs, B. (1976) *Freedom and Liberation*, Sussex University Press.

Gibson, M. (1977) "Rationality", *Philosophy and Public Affairs*, Vol. 6, pp. 193–225.

Girvetz, H. (1963) *The Evolution of Liberalism*, (rev. edn.), Stanford University Press.

Gordon, S. (1976) "The new contractarians", *Journal of Political Economy*, Vol. 84, pp. 573–90.

——(1980) *Welfare, Justice and Freedom*, Columbia University Press.

Griffin, J. (1977) "Are there incommensurable values? ", *Philosophy and Public Affairs*, Vol. 7, pp. 39–59.

Hamlin, A. P. (1983) "Procedural individualism and outcome liberalism", *Scottish Journal of Political Economy*, Vol. 30, pp. 251–63.

——(1984a) "Constitutional control of processes and their outcomes", *Public Choice*, Vol. 42, pp. 13–45.

——(1984b) "Public choice, markets and utilitarianism", in Whynes, D. K. (ed.) (1984) *What is Political Economy?* Basil Blackwell.

Hammond, P. J. (1981) "Ex-ante and ex-post welfare optimality under uncertainty", *Economica*, Vol. 48, pp. 235–50.

Hammond, P. J. (1982) "Utilitarianism, uncertainty and information", in Sen, A. K. and Williams, B. A. O. (eds.) (1982) *Utilitarianism and Beyond*, Cambridge University Press.

Hare, R. M. (1976) "Ethical theory and utilitarianism". Reprinted in Sen, A. K. and Williams, B.A.O. (eds.) (1982) *Utilitarianism and Beyond*, Cambridge University Press.

Harrison, R. (ed.) (1979) *Rational Action*, Cambridge University Press.

Harsanyi, J. C. (1953) "Cardinal utility in welfare economics and in the theory of risk taking", *Journal of Political Economy*, Vol. 61, pp. 434-45. Reprinted in Harsanyi, J. C. (1976).

——(1955) "Cardinal welfare, individualistic ethics and interpersonal comparisons of utility", *Journal of Political Economy*, Vol. 63, pp. 309–21. Reprinted in Harsanyi, J. C. (1976).

——(1975a) "Can the maximinum principle serve as a basis for morality? A critique of John Rawls' theory", *American Political Science Review*, Vol. 59, pp. 594–606.

——(1975b) "Nonlinear social welfare functions: do welfare economists have a special exemption from Bayesian rationality? ", *Theory and Decision*, Vol. 6, pp. 311–32. Reprinted in Harsanyi, J. C. (1976).

——(1976) *Essays in Ethics, Social behaviour and Scientific Explantion*, D. Reidel, Dordrecht.

——(1977) "Morality and the theory of rational behaviour", *Social Research*, Vol. 44, No. 4. Reprinted in Sen, A. K. and Williams, B. A. O. (eds.) (1982) *Utilitarianism and Beyond*, Cambridge University Press.

——(1978) "Bayesian decision theory and utilitarian ethics", *American Economic Review*, Vol. 68, pp. 223–8.

——(1980) "Rule utilitarianism, rights, obligations and the theory of rational behaviour", *Theory and Decision*, Vol. 12, pp. 115–33.

Hayek, F. A. (1960) *The Constitution of Liberty*, University of Chicago Press.

——(1973, 1976, 1979) *Law, Legislation and Liberty* (3 Vols.), University of Chicago Press.

Hohfeld, W. (1923) *Fundamental Legal Conceptions*, Yale University Press.

Hollis, M. (1979) "Rational man and social science", in Harrison, R. (ed.) (1979).

Hollis, M. and Nell, E. (1975) *Rational Economic Man*, Cambridge University Press.

Hollis, M. and Lukes, S. (eds.) (1982) *Rationality and Relativism*, Basil Blackwell.

Honderich, E. (1976) *Three Essays on Political Violence*, Basil Blackwell.

Howe, R. E. and Roemer, J. E. (1981) "Rawlsian justice as the core of a game", *American Economic Review*, Vol. 71, pp. 880–95.

Husami, Z. I. (1978) "Marx on distributive justice", *Philosophy and Public Affairs*, Vol. 8, pp. 27–64.

Kahneman, D. and Tversky, A. (1979) "Prospect theory: an analysis of decision under risk", *Econometrica*, Vol. 47, pp. 263–91.

Kreps, D., Milgrom, P., Roberts, J. and Wilson, R. (1982) "Rational cooperation in the finitely repeated prisoners' dilemma, *Journal of Economic Theory*, Vol. 27, pp. 245–52.

Landes, W. M. and Posner, R. A. (1975) "The independent judiciary in an interest-group perspective", *Journal of Law and Economics*, Vol. 18, pp. 875–901.

Loasby, B. J. (1976) *Choice, Complexity and Ignorance*, Cambridge University Press.

Loomes, G. and Sugden, R. (1982) "Regret theory: an alternative theory of rational choice under uncertainty", *Economic Journal*, Vol. 92, pp. 805–24.

Luce, R. D. and Raiffa, H. (1957) *Games and Decision*, J. Wiley and Sons.

Lyons, D. (1965) *Forms and Limits of Utilitarianism*, Oxford University Press.

——(1980) "Utility as a possible ground of rights", *Nous*, Vol. 14, pp. 17–28.

Machina, M. J. (1982) "Expected utility analysis without the independence axiom", *Econometrica*, Vol. 50, pp. 277–323.

Mackie, J. L. (1977) *Ethics: Inventing Right and Wrong*, Pelican.

Macpherson, C. B. (1978) "The meaning of property", in Macpherson, C. B. (ed.) (1978) *Property: Mainstream and Critical Positions*, University of Toronto Press.

Margolis, H. (1982) *Selfishness, Altruism and Rationality*, Cambridge University Press.

Marschak, J. (1950) "Rational behaviour, uncertain prospects and measurable utility", *Econometrica*, Vol. 18, pp. 111–41.

Maynard-Smith, J. (1973) *On Evolution*, Edinburgh University Press.

Mill, J. S. (1910) *On Liberty*, Everyman.

Minogue, K. (1963) *The Liberal Mind*, Methuen.

Mirrlees, J. A. (1982) "The economic uses of utilitarianism", in Sen, A. K. and Williams, B. A. O. (eds.) (1982) *Utilitarianism and Beyond*, Cambridge University Press.

Morishima, M. (1974) *Marx's Economics*, Cambridge University Press.

Mueller, D. C. (1979) *Public Choice*, Cambridge University Press.

Nagel, T. (1970) *The Probability of Altruism*, Oxford University Press.

Nath, S. K. (1969) *A Reappraisal of Welfare Economics*, Routledge and Kegan Paul.

Niskanen, W. A. (1971) *Bureaucracy and Representative Government*, Aldine-Atherton.

Norman, R. (1971) *Reasons for Action*, Basil Blackwell.

Nozick, R. (1974) *Anarchy, State and Utopia*, Basic Books.

Olson, M. (1965) *The Logic of Collective Action*, Harvard University Press.

Parfit, D. (1973) "Later selves and moral principles", in Montefiore, A. (ed.) (1973) *Philosophy and Personal Relations*, Routledge and Kegan Paul.

——(1979) "Prudence, morality and the prisoners' dilemma", *Proceedings of the British Academy*, Vol. 65, pp. 539–64.

——(1984) *Reasons and Persons*, Oxford University Press.

Peffer, R. (1978) "A defence of rights to well-being", *Philosophy and Public Affairs*, Vol. 8, pp. 65–87.

Phelps, E. (ed.) (1975) *Altruism, Morality and Economic Theory*, Russell Sage Foundation.

Ramsey, F. P. (1928) "A mathematical theory of saving", *Economic Journal*, Vol. 38, pp. 543–59.

Rawls, J. (1971) *A Theory of Justice*, Harvard University Press.

Reiman, J. H. (1981) "The fallacy of libertarian capitalism", *Ethics*, Vol. 92, pp. 85–95.

Roemer, J. E. (1980) "A general equilibrium approach to Marxian economics", *Econometrica*, Vol. 48, pp. 505–30.

——(1982a) "Property relations vs surplus value in Marxian exploitation", *Philosophy and Public Affairs*, Vol. 11, pp. 281–313.

——(1982b) "Origins of exploitation and class: value theory of pre-capitalist economy", *Econometrica*, Vol. 50, pp. 163–92.

——(1982c) *A general Theory of Exploitation and Class*, Harvard University Press.

——(1982d) "Exploitation, alternatives and socialism", *Economic Journal*, Vol. 92, pp. 87–107.

Rowley, C. and Peacock, A. (1975) *Welfare Economics: A Liberal Restatement*, Martin Robertson.

Runciman, W. G. and Sen, A. K. (1965) "Games, justice and the general will", *Mind*, Vol. 74, pp. 554–62.

Sandel, M. (1982) *Liberalism and the Limits of Justice*, Cambridge University Press.

Sandel, M. (ed.) (1984) *Liberalism and its Critics*, Basil Blackwell.

Scanlon, T. M. (1982) "Contractualism and utilitarianism", in Sen, A. K. and Williams, B. A. O. (eds.) (1982) *Utilitarianism and Beyond*, Cambridge University Press.

Schelling, T. C. (1960) *The Strategy of Conflict*, Harvard University Press.

——(1978) *Micromotives and Macrobehaviour*, Norton.

——(1980) "The intimate contest for self command", in McMurrin, S. M. (ed.) *The Tanner Lectures on Human Values IV*, University of Utah Press. Reprinted in Schelling (1984).

——(1984) *Choice and Consequence*, Harvard University Press.

Schoemaker, P. J. H. (1982) "The expected utility model: its variants, purposes, evidence and limitations", *Journal of Economic Literature*, Vol. 20, pp. 529–63.

Schotter, A. (1981) *The Economic Theory of Social Institutions*, Cambridge University Press.

Sen, A. K. (1967) "Isolation, assurance and the social rate of discount", *Quarterly Journal of Economics*, Vol. 81, pp. 112–25.

——(1970) "The impossibility of a Paretian liberal", *Journal of Political Economy*, Vol. 78, pp. 152–7.

——(1973) *On Economic Inequality*, Oxford University Press.

——(1974) "Choice, orderings and morality", in Körner, S. (ed.) (1974) *Practical Reason*, Oxford University Press.

——(1976) "Liberty, unanimity and rights", *Economica*, Vol. 43, pp. 217–45.

——(1977) "Rational fools: a critique of the behavioural foundations of economic theory", *Philosophy and Public Affairs*, Vol. 6, pp. 317–44.

——(1979a) "Personal utilities and public judgements: or what's wrong with welfare economics", *Economic Journal*, Vol. 89, pp. 537–58.

——(1979b) "Utilitarianism and welfarism", *Journal of Philosophy*, Vol. 76, pp. 463–89.

——(1982) "Rights and agency", *Philosophy and Public Affairs*, Vol. 11, pp. 3–39.

——(1983) "Poor, relatively speaking", *Oxford Economic Papers*, Vol. 35, pp. 153–69.

Sen, A. K. and Williams, B. A. O. (eds.) (1982) *Utilitarianism and Beyond*, Cambridge University Press.

Shackle, G. L. S. (1972) *Epistemics and Economics*, Cambridge University Press.

Shubik, M. (1982) *Game Theory in the Social Sciences*, MIT Press.

Sidgwick, H. (1907) *The Method of Ethics* (7th edn.) Macmillan.

Simon, H. A., (1954), "A behavioural theory of rational choice", *Quarterly Journal of Economics*, Vol. 69, pp. 99–118.

——(1976) "From substantive to procedural rationality", in Latsis, S. (ed.) (1976) *Method and Appraisal in Economics*, Cambridge University Press.

——(1978a) "Rationality as process and as product of thought", *American Economic Review*, Vol. 68, pp. 1–16.

———(1978b) "On how to decide what to do", *Bell Journal of Economics*, Vol. 9, pp. 494–507.

———(1983) *Reason in Human Affairs*, Basil Blackwell.

Smart, J. J. C., and Williams, B. A. O. (eds.) (1973) *Utilitarianism: For and Against*, Cambridge University Press.

Strotz, R. (1955) Myopia and inconsistency in dynamic utility maximisation", *Review of Economic Studies*, Vol. 23, pp. 165–80.

Sugden, R. (1982) "On the economics of philanthropy" *Economic Journal*, Vol. 92, pp. 341–50.

———(1984) Reciprocity: the supply of public goods through voluntary contributions", *Economic Journal*, Vol. 94, pp. 772–87.

Taylor, C. (1982) "Rationality", in Hollis and Lukes (eds.) (1982).

Taylor, M. (1982) *Community, Anarchy and Liberty*, Cambridge University Press.

Ullmann-Margalit, E. (1977) *The Emergence of Norms*, Oxford University Press.

Ulph, A. M. (1982) "The role of ex ante and ex post decisions in the valuation of life", *Journal of Public Economics*, Vol. 18, pp. 265–76.

Weizsacker, C. C. von (1971) "Notes on endogenous change of tastes", *Journal of economic theory*, Vol. 3, pp. 345–72.

Whynes, D. K. and Bowles, R. A. (1981) *The Economic Theory of the State*, Martin Robertson.

Williams, B. A. O. (1972) *Morality: An Introduction to Ethics*, Harper and Row.

Williamson, O. E. (1975) *Markets and Hierarchies: Analysis and Antitrust Implication*, The Free Press.

Wilson, B. R. (ed.) (1970) *Rationality*, Basil Blackwell.

Winch, P. (1964) "Understanding a primitive society", *American Philosophical Quarterly*, Vol. 1, pp. 307–24.

Winter, S. G. (1964) "Economic natural selection and the theory of the firm", *Yale Economic Essays*, Vol. 4, 225–72.

Wolff, R. P. (1970) *In Defense of Anarchism*, Harper and Row.

———(1981) "A critique and reinterpretation of Marx's labour theory of value", *Philosophy and Public Affairs*, Vol. 10, pp. 89–120.

Wood, A. W. (1972) "The Marxian critique of justice", *Philosophy and Public Affairs*, Vol. 1, pp. 244–82.

———(1979) "Marx on right and justice: a reply to Husami", *Philosophy and Public Affairs*, Vol. 8, pp. 267–95.

Index

194